CLASSROOM KICKOFF

Written and Edited
by
Linda Milliken

Illustrated
by
Barb Lorseyedi
Priscilla Burris

Typography
by
Lorraine Stegman

ISBN 1-56472-001-2

Classroom Kickoff • Edupress • ©1991
P.O. Box 883, Dana Point, CA 92629

Classroom Kickoff

Table of Contents

Let's Get Organized/Teacher

Useful organization ideas, tips and tools to help you run an efficient classroom and make planning easier.

Let's Get Organized/Students

Activities and projects that help students learn about organizing and how to actually implement it in their lives.

Marvelous Motivators

Awards, notes and motivation programs at your fingertips to inspire, reward and excite your students.

Parents are Partners

Tips, forms, conference checklists and more to simplify home-school communication and involve parents in their child's education.

Bulletin Board Library

Teach, motivate and share with bulletin board displays that you and your students can easily create.

Classroom Kickoff

Table of Contents

Art Start

Brighten your classroom with art projects that leave creativity to the kids! Easy preparation allows you extra time to interact with your students.

Just for Openers

Innovative ways to start each day. Includes a variety of independent activities and routines. Learning will take place while you're free to take care of those necessary morning clerical details.

Tips from Teachers

Super tips sent in by our network of super teacher!

Start it in September

Projects that start in September—or any time—and continue throughout the year will get kids looking ahead with excitement and make year-long planning a snap.

Get Going with Games

Games to fill spare moments, rainy days and recesses all year long.

Classroom Kickoff

Table of Contents

Project Planner

Awaras, notes and motivation programs at your fingertips to inspire, reward and excite your students.

Group Effort

Involve students in co-operative learning activities that will teach them the value of working together.

Write Right Away

A bundle of writing topics and activities designed to break the "writing ice" and involve students in a year-long writing program.

Let's Talk

Tips and topics for positive communication. Set the tone for sharing, understanding and problem-solving together.

Theme Weeks

Ten themes—one for each month of the school year—and five activities—one for each day of the week—to keep the theme alive.

Classroom Kickoff

Table of Contents

Instant Activity

Reproducible activity pages for seatwork at a moment's notice. Thought-provoking and fun, too—filled with challenges at all levels of thinking.

Month by Month

Need a curriculum spark? Look here for a monthly roundup of holidays and happenings that will serve as springboards for planning creative, change-of-pace lessons.

Information Inventory

A super resource of book lists, addresses and useful information at your fingertips.

Clip-Art Creativity

An ample supply of boxes, borders and illustrations—just cut and paste your way to designer notes, awards and seatwork.

Index

Looking for something in particular? Check the index.
A great time-saving feature just for you.

The Year at a Glance

For a long-term look at the school year, use this page as a planning tool for curriculum goals, special events or thematic units.

August	September	October
November	December	January
February	March	April
May	June	July

CLASSROOM KICKOFF • © EDUPRESS

Lesson Plan ✔Checklist

Have you ever started a lesson and realized you didn't have everything that you needed? Or finished a lesson and realized you didn't accomplish what you had intended?

This checklist should help remedy those problems. Keep some handy while you are planning your school week. Even if you don't complete a checklist for every lesson you can mentally run through the information.

✔Objective

✔Plan/Procedure

✔Pretest   yes ☐   no ☐   **✔Prior learning skills necessary:**

✔Advance preparation:

✔Teacher materials: **✔Student materials:**

✔Follow-up assignments and due dates
   Class: **Homework:**

✔Instructional Follow-up/Evaluation
   Posttest   yes ☐   no ☐
   Students needing additional help:

   Additional lessons required:

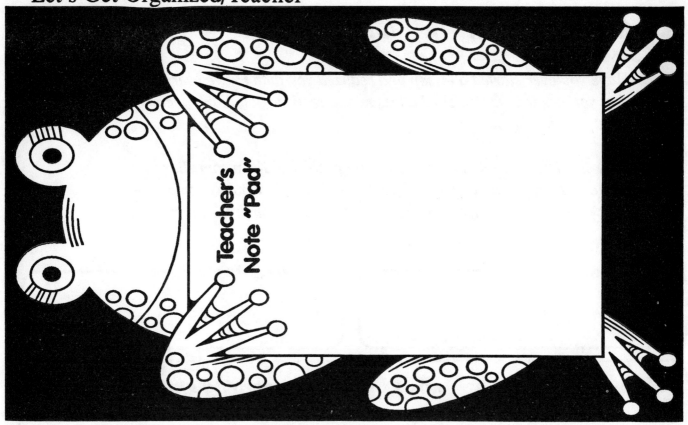

Teacher's Note "Pad"

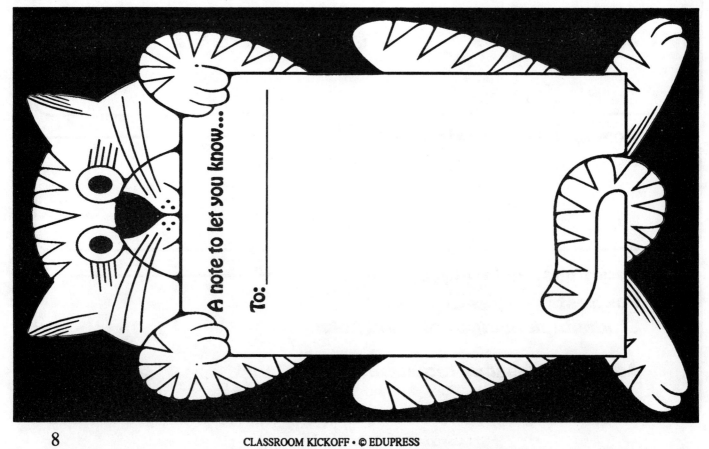

A note to let you know...

To: _____

Mini-Note Messages

*Keeping in touch with parents and students can easily be accomplished if you keep a stack of **mini-note messages** ready for quick reminders and words of encouragement.*

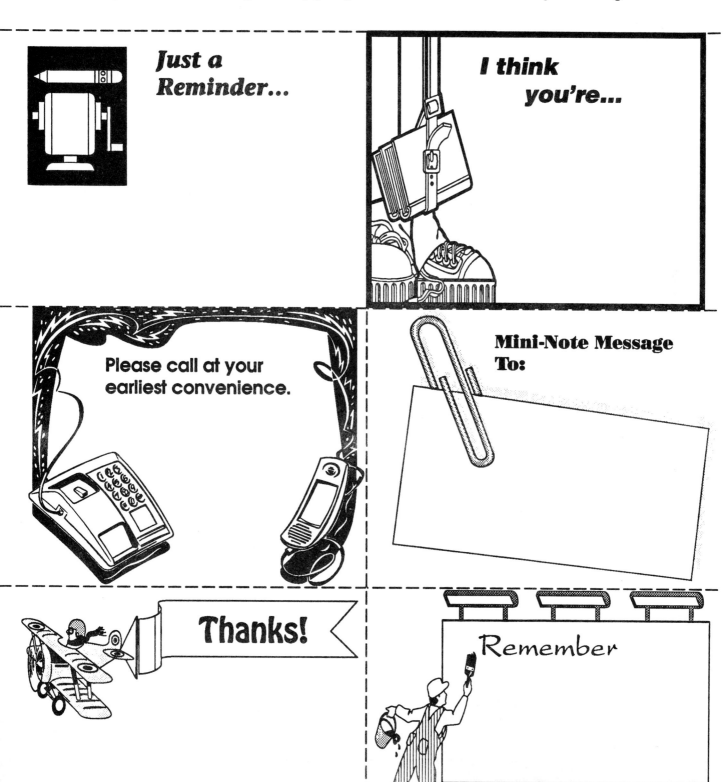

Just a Reminder...

I think you're...

Please call at your earliest convenience.

Mini-Note Message To:

Thanks!

Remember

Handy-Dandy Class List

> *A master list of students in your class comes in handy for a variety of uses.*
> *Update the list when needed and keep extra copies in a box on your desk.*

Student use:

✎ Name games (see pages 248, 249)

✎ Friendship events

✎ Study partners, homework help–Students can keep a list of phone numbers at home. They'll always have someone to call with a question about an assignment or project.

✎ Valentine and other holiday card exchanges.

✎ Note writing.

Teacher use:

✎ *Accountability*–Check off names as children bring in required notes, permission slips, forms and assignments.

✎ *Grouping*—Use different colored highlighting pens to indicate committee members, reading and math groups. Post one copy for students to see and keep one copy in your plan book for quick and easy reference. Highlight names to let parent aides know which students they will be helping.

✎ *Record keeping*—Use as a checklist for extra credit work, overdue library books, citizenship points.

✎ *Job assignments*—Provide a color key to indicate a classroom responsibility. For example, a name highlighted in yellow is responsible for emptying the trash that week.

✎ *Instant list*— Fill requests easily for name lists from parent organizations or student council.

Student Class List

Teacher: _____ **Room #:** _____

1. _____
2. _____
3. _____
4. _____
5. _____
6. _____
7. _____
8. _____
9. _____
10. _____
11. _____
12. _____
13. _____
14. _____
15. _____
16. _____
17. _____
18. _____
19. _____
20. _____
21. _____
22. _____
23. _____
24. _____
25. _____
26. _____
27. _____
28. _____
29. _____
30. _____
31. _____
32. _____
33. _____
34. _____

Volunteer Summary
(✔) if prefer work at home

Parent resources can be extremely valuable, if you know who, how and where to get the help.

Send the volunteer request letter (following page) home with your students. Summarize the responses on this form.

Keep the summary handy so you will know just who to call for the assistance you need.

Field trips:

Library aide:

Correcting papers, typing:

Art preparation:

Helping at parties or special days:

Baking or sending food for special events:

Supplying materials for special events:

Telephoning:

Special skill to share or teach: (include skill after name)

Speaker:

Calling all volunteers!

SCHOOL

We would love to have you participate in our classroom "family."

Even if you work, you can still be involved!

Please take time to indicate ways you would be willing to help by checking the boxes below.

Return the form with your child as soon as possible. Thank you.

Name(s) _____

- ☐ field trips
- ☐ library help
- ☐ art preparation at home or school (circle choice)
- ☐ working with students in class
- ☐ correcting papers at home or school (circle choice)
- ☐ baking for parties and special days
- ☐ helping at parties and on special days
- ☐ supplying items for special days, projects, events
- ☐ telephoning from home
- ☐ teaching or sharing a skill or occupation with students (list skill or occupation)

Stock Your Art Cupboard

Don't be like Old Mother Hubbard! A well-stocked art cupboard will help you in more ways than you imagined. It's a real time-saver when preparing art and craft lessons. It's a life-saver for rainy days when you need to keep restless students constructively occupied. And it's a real help-mate when it's time to plan your lessons, special days and bulletin boards. Just *looking* inside the brimming closet should put loads of ideas into your head for creative, fun-filled projects.

But how do you go about filling this empty space? Well, think about basic art needs. These should be supplied by the school. Be sure that your art cupboard includes:

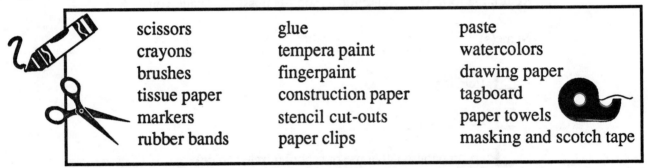

scissors	glue	paste
crayons	tempera paint	watercolors
brushes	fingerpaint	drawing paper
tissue paper	construction paper	tagboard
markers	stencil cut-outs	paper towels
rubber bands	paper clips	masking and scotch tape

Now add a wide variety of supplies that will add to the dimension of your students' art experiences.

Where will you get all these things . . . and more? From PARENTS, of course. And that will be easy. Use the letter on the following page and follow three easy steps.

1. Make two copies, one for your file.

2. On the second copy, ✓ the items you would like donated.

3. Reproduce the letter to send home with each student.

Be ready to get that cupboard filled! Running low in February? Get out your master list, check the needed items and send the letter home again.

Extra Tips

▶ Be sure one of your class helper positions is **ART CUPBOARD MONITOR.**
▶ Keep an inventory sheet posted on the door . Don't count on your memory to know what is in the far back corner of the bottom shelf!
▶ Keep extra boxes for crayon scraps, tissue scraps and construction paper scraps.
▶ **DON'T THROW ANYTHING AWAY!** It just might be a future work of art!
▶ It's always a good idea to include newspapers, rags, paint shirts, sponges and any other things that will make clean up easier.

Dear Parents,

We're busy stocking our art cupboard so we will always be prepared for some imaginative learning. Will you help us? We're counting on you to take our cupboard from **BARE to BEAUTIFUL!**

Please look at the list below. If you can send any of the items I have checked to school with your child we will be very grateful!

❑ EVERYTHING

❑ wire	❑ popcorn	❑ drinking straws	❑ used greeting cards
❑ TV dinner trays	❑ wire hangers	❑ food coloring	❑ styrofoam meat trays
❑ bars of soap	❑ liquid soap	❑ Ivory soap flakes	❑ mail order catalogs
❑ dried beans	❑ wallpaper samples	❑ paper towel rolls	❑ bathroom tissue rolls
❑ shoe boxes	❑ gift boxes, any size	❑ marbles	❑ toothpicks
❑ pop-top tabs	❑ giftwrap	❑ margarine tubs	❑ plastic milk containers
❑ egg cartons	❑ buttons	❑ ribbons, bows	❑ plastic 6-pack holder
❑ aluminum foil	❑ waxed paper	❑ fabric remnants	❑ small wood scraps
❑ carpet samples	❑ wood doweling	❑ yarn	❑ string
❑ rubber bands	❑ pipe cleaners	❑ zip-lock baggies	❑ plastic forks, spoons
❑ rope	❑ markers	❑ sandpaper	❑ shower curtain rings
❑ safety pins	❑ marbles	❑ brown lunch sacks	❑ paper plates, cups
❑ brads	❑ balloons	❑ empty thread spools	❑ empty film canisters
❑ twist ties	❑ sponges	❑ assorted pasta	❑ magazines
❑ newspaper	❑ baby food jars	❑ clear, spray lacquer	❑ coffee cans, lids
❑ raffia	❑ junk jewelry	❑ paint stirrers	❑ felt squares & scraps
❑ popsicle sticks	❑ puffy paints	❑ stencils & transfers	❑ rick-rack & trims
❑ felt	❑ burlap	❑ fiberfill	❑ lace

OTHER:_____

_____

Please do not send anything you want returned. We plan on using it ALL!

Thank you.

Special Schedules

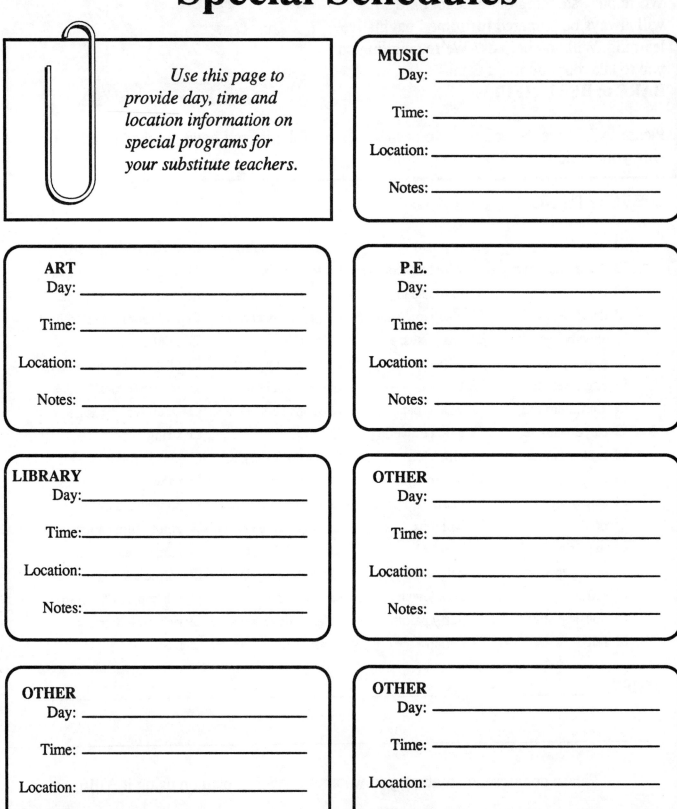

Use this page to provide day, time and location information on special programs for your substitute teachers.

MUSIC
Day: _____

Time: _____

Location: _____

Notes: _____

ART
Day: _____

Time: _____

Location: _____

Notes: _____

P.E.
Day: _____

Time: _____

Location: _____

Notes: _____

LIBRARY
Day: _____

Time: _____

Location: _____

Notes: _____

OTHER
Day: _____

Time: _____

Location: _____

Notes: _____

OTHER
Day: _____

Time: _____

Location: _____

Notes: _____

OTHER
Day: _____

Time: _____

Location: _____

Notes: _____

For my substitute teacher…

Welcome to my class! I hope this information will help make your day easier.

Faculty information

Principal:

Secretary:

Classroom aides:

Helpful teachers:

Where to find

Art materials:

Paper:

Student helper chart:

Other:

Fire drill

Location of exit map:

General procedure:

Helpful students

Daily Schedule

Teacher's hours:_____ to _____

Students arrive: _____

Classes begin: _____

Classes end: _____

Recess: _____ _____

Lunch: _____ to _____

Duty: _____

Student pull-outs for special programs

Music: Speech:

Reading: Other:

Students with health problems, limited phys. ed., etc.

Discipline/problem students

It's Back to School Again...

It's Back-to-School night again. We've gathered some ideas from teachers and provided you with a planning checklist to help the evening run smoothly! . Good Luck!

Prepare for Them...

Your room should look inviting!
Try...
- ...**decorating** with lots of color
- ...**displaying** student-created art and writing
- ...**cleaning** desktops
- ...**designing** a student-made welcome sign for the door
- ...**marking** each student's desk

Introduce Them...

People are important!
Introduce...
- ...**yourself**—Review your teaching experience and philosophy. Describe your interests and background.
- ...**classroom aides**— what help is needed?
- ...**principals, secretaries** and other **school personnel**—Discuss ways they can assist.
- ...**your students**—share your impressions of the students and the class as a whole.

Inform Them...

Familiarize parents with the curriculum.
Tell them about...
- ...**reading, writing** and **spelling** programs
- ...**social studies** and **science** curriculum
- ...**math** objectives
- ...**music** and **art** opportunities
- ...**support systems**—specialists, speech pathologists, labs
- ...**computer** instruction

Interest them...

Parents like to picture their children in school.
Show them...
- ...**a map** of school and classroom
- ...**a schedule** of daily events
- ...**special centers** and **activity areas**
- ...**procedures** for turning in work, free time activities
- ...**sample** group **lessons**

Involve Them...

Let parents know you want them as educational partners.
Explain to them...
- ...**homework** policy
- ...**discipline** methods
- ...**communication** plan—newsletters, notes
- ...**conference** schedules
- ...your **"office hours"** —the best time to reach you for a conversation or appointment
- ...your need for **parent volunteers**

It's Back to School Again

Here are some teacher-shared ideas for making Back-to-School night more memorable for parents and more relaxed for you!

Ice Breakers

Start with a simple game—try to match parents with students.

Let parents design and wear their own name tags.

Take a group picture.

Conduct a mock opening…call roll, salute the flag, take care of your usual school business.

Read a favorite story aloud.

Hand out tickets for door prizes—student-made drawings or craft (The kids will love doing this *and* hearing the results!)

SIGN IN Please!

Ask students to decorate the door with a large sheet of butcher paper for parents to sign when they arrive.

Involve parents in a **"cookie graph"**. Provide a plate of several different cookies and ask them to graph their favorite. Share the results with students the next day.

Have parents color a simple picture to tape to their child's desk as a way of saying "I was here."

It's Back to School Again

Designer Presentations

Present a slide show of classroom activities—narrated by students.

"Run" parents through a condensed version of a school day. Stop along the way to explain curriculum and show supplemental materials.

Provide "handouts", with student illustrations, so parents can follow along.

Have children draw pictures on clear laminate to correspond with your presentation. Show the pictures on an overhead projector as you present your information.

Ask students to create puppets for you to use during your presentation … My teacher, Mr. Math, Science Wizard, Reading Robot etc.

Have students tape messages to the parents to play intermittently during your talk.

Set up mini-centers that display your instructional program. Rotate parents through the centers.

Make a video tape to show.

In Closing

It's over! How do you avoid the parents' urge for a mini-conference right then and there?

Provide an appointment slip for parents to complete. Let them know you will followup with a call to discuss their questions and concerns.

Ask them to complete a simple survey that gives you more information about their child. Show them where to "turn it in" as they leave.

Set up a table of recommended books you'd like to share with them. Divert their attention to the books rather than individual student discussions.

Planning for OPEN HOUSE

OPEN HOUSE is a night parents and students always look forward to. But it requires a lot of planning and preparation! Hopefully, these ideas will provide inspiration and save valuable time!

PLANNING HINTS

Decide on a theme, if any, for this special night. For example ...

Little Classroom on the Prairie   **Back to Nature**   **Color Celebrations**

Plan integrated activities based on the theme.

Draw a mini-map of the classroom and decide **what** you want to display and **where**.

Make a complete list, well in advance, of *"things to do"*.

DISPLAY IDEAS

Include a lot of color.

Hang student artwork from the ceiling.

Represent all curriculum areas in the displays.

Desktops should have a writing folder, art portfolio, or other compendium of student creations.

COMMUNICATE

Provide plenty of advance notice for families to plan for the evening.

Include the date in your monthly newsletter.

Send home a *personal* letter.

Send home student-created invitations.

ON TOUR

Prepare a map of the room. Point out where and what they will see and the order, if any, you would like them to see it in. (This can help traffic through the room if you have a large attendance.)

Create a written program. Relate a short story, background information about what they will see.

Train your students to be *tour guides*. Have them plan ahead of time, what they want to show and tell.

THAT NIGHT

Involve parents. Instead of the standard sign-in, ask them for feedback, too. "What did you like the best?" "Any messages about what you saw that you would like to share with the students?"

Plan a student demonstration. Be sure it is one they don't *have to* be there for. Choral reading or a simple non-partner folk dance work well. (This may increase attendance.)

JUST FOR FUN

Hang student self-portraits from the ceiling over the desk.

Stuff life-size butcher paper students, dressed in their own clothing, to sit in chairs.

Award a prize to the 25th person through the door. (Have them take a numbered ticket when they come in.)

FOLLOW-UP

Write a personal thank you note to parents who attended.

Ask students to write a thank you note to their parents, too.

Read the parent comments from the guest book to the students.

Share stories and parent comments. Everyone will enjoy the positive feedback!

Let's Get Organized/Teacher

Student Name _____

Record your observations and evaluation of individual reading abilities on this form.

Then use the form as a discussion guide for both parent and student conferences.

Interests:

Strengths:

Weaknesses:

Suggestions and Strategies:

Student Goal:

Teacher Goal:

Parent Goal:

Conference Dates:

Let's Get Organized!

Create bulletin boards that stay up year-round to remind students of upcoming important dates and events. Here are two ideas.

Elephants never forget!

Cut out a large elephant head and trunk. Glue peanuts to clothespins then Velcro the clothespins to the bulletin board. Clip reminders written on index cards to the clothespin.

A string around the finger is a good way to remember something important. Dip string in fabric stiffener. When dry, tie lengths into bows. Post reminders inside each loop.

Free-Time Fillers

> *"Now what can I do?"*
> *The assignment is finished. Other students are still busy working. What now?*

Develop an activity box for your students.

Fill it with an assortment of fun-filled activities such as interesting magazines, mazes, coloring sheets, word search and puzzles. Keep the activities "reward-related". It should be a special treat for the students who have finished their work to go to the activity box. Change the activities to relate to the time of year or approaching holiday.

Increase student interest and excitement by decorating the box and relating the activities with a monthly theme.

HOLIDAY THEMES

Tape a Halloween pumpkin to the front of a **TREATS FOR YOU** box.
Put activities inside a huge **SANTA'S SPECIAL STOCKING**.
Cover a **LEPRECHAUN'S POT OF GOLD** with gold foil paper.

SPECIAL THEMES

Create a pirate's **TREASURE CHEST**.
Stuff a box of **MONSTROUS FUN** with activities about mysteries and monsters.
Create a **TIME MACHINE** from a box and fill it with past and future fun.

STUDENT CLASSROOM CALENDAR

Here's a school calendar to help you plan and organize. List important assignments, things to remember, special events and holidays. Keep the calendar in your notebook.

Month _____

Monday	Tuesday	Wednesday	Thursday	Friday

Let's Get Organized/Students

Desk Organizing Tips   (Teacher note: Reproduce a copy for each student. Cut apart.)

If you keep your desk neat and organized you will discover that it is easier to be more organized about your *school assignments*. Being able to find things easily is a real time saver!

Here are some tips to help you keep your desk "in order". Cut them out and put them in your notebook as a reminder.

1. **Pick a day**—Tuesday, for example—clean out your desk during free time on that day each week.

2. **Keep** crayons, markers and paper clips **separated** in clearly marked boxes or bags.

3. **Sort through your papers** every day. Take home whatever your parents are supposed to see. Throw away scraps and extra papers.

4. **Don't keep anything** in your desk that **doesn't** help with school assignments.

5. **Don't keep valuable** things in your desk.

6. **Arrange your books** by size, schedule or subject—then keep them that way.

- -

Daily Schedule

Complete this daily school schedule and tape it to your desk. Fill in the clocks with the correct hand positions. Keep an eye on the *classroom* clock and allow enough time to complete your work, get ready for the next lesson, or clean up for recess.

Subject	Start	End	Subject	Start	End

Personalized Storage

Here are two ways to help students keep track of school supplies that wind up scattered in the bottom of a desk or lying on the floor. Projects can progress much faster if kids learn to keep their "tools" organized and easy to get to.

Keep scissors, crayons, glue, pencils, rulers and other supplies in these storage containers. If they don't fit inside the desks keep them handy on top or in an art cabinet.

My Box

Cut out pictures of "favorites" from magazines. Include such things as sports, foods, colors, pets and clothing.

Paint the pictures on a shoebox with a diluted mixture of water and glue. Completely cover the box and its lid.

Write your name on a strip of masking tape on the lid.

My Bag

Personalize a large ziptop freezer bag to hold school items.

To decorate, cut strips of masking tape and put them on the bag in a pattern or design.

Use crayons or markers to color the tape.

Write your name in bold letters across a strip of tape at the top of the bag.

O.K.!! Organizing for Kids

Organizing is a fact of life! Whether you do it well already or need to learn some easy, painless ways to get yourself organized, the fact is that when you're organized you know where things are, you're ready on time, and things in your life are more orderly. Let's start with some easy organizing that every kid, even *you*, can handle successfully!

Here's a typical dresser crammed with stuff—socks, underwear, pajamas, sweats, shirts, blouses, sweaters, jewelry, hats, earmuffs, scarves, gloves, mittens, etc.

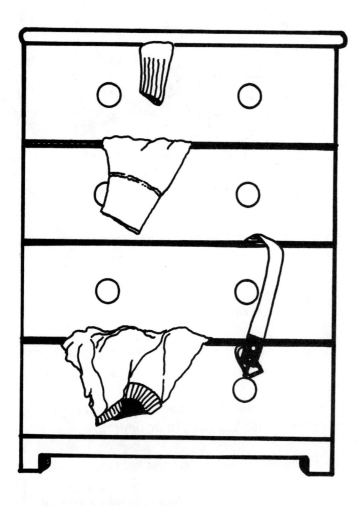

The problem is that although you have plenty of space for all your things, you can't find anything easily. Your socks are unsorted, there's a blue belt in one drawer and a black one in another. One glove is in a jacket pocket and the other is in your top drawer. In general, things in this dresser are a mess and can't be easily found.

Let's get organized!

On the following page is an illustration of a four-drawer dresser and a picture "list" of items for the dresser. Cut out the pictures and glue them on each drawer so that the dresser will be organized.

Have fun and let's see who can be the most organized!

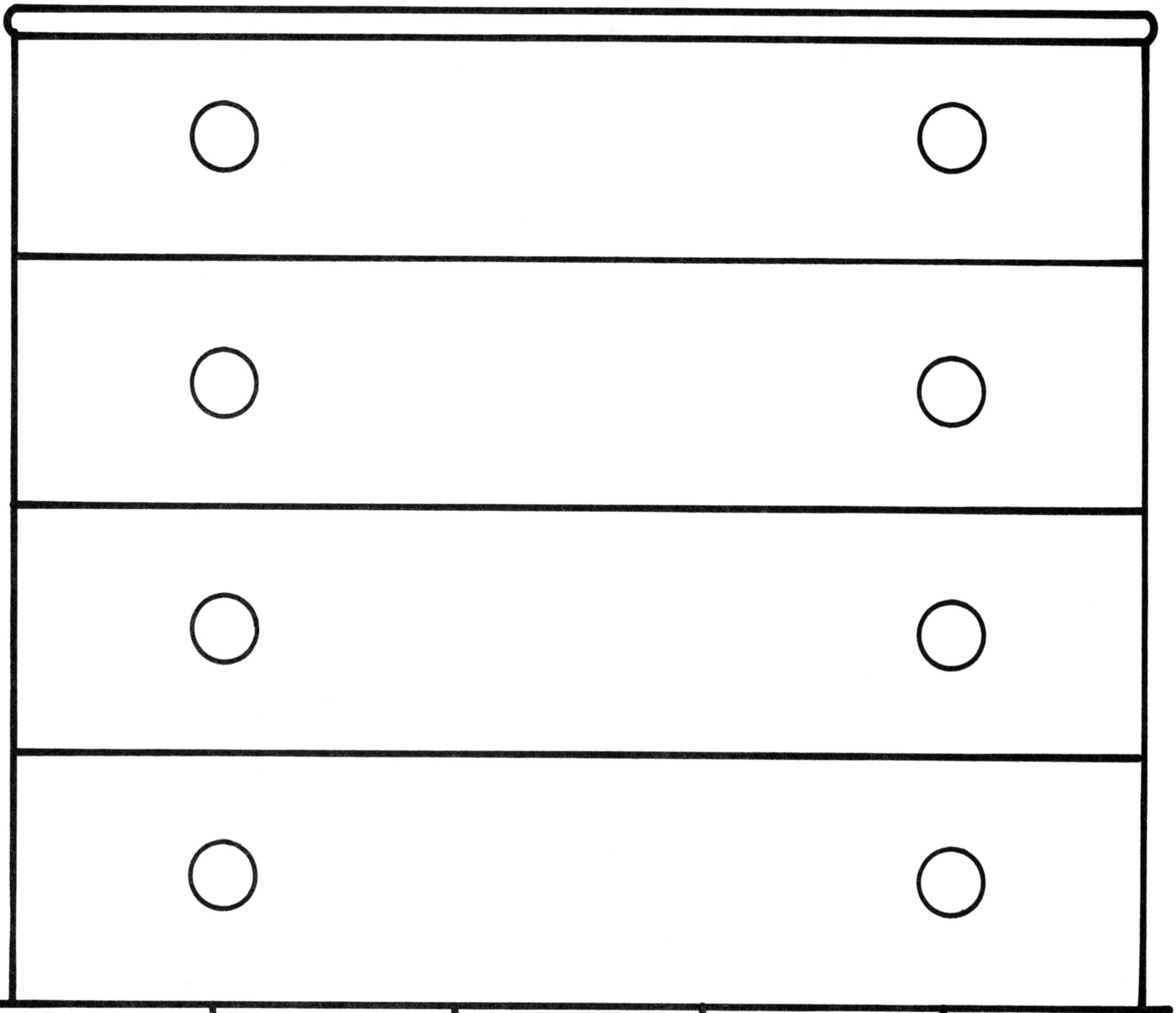

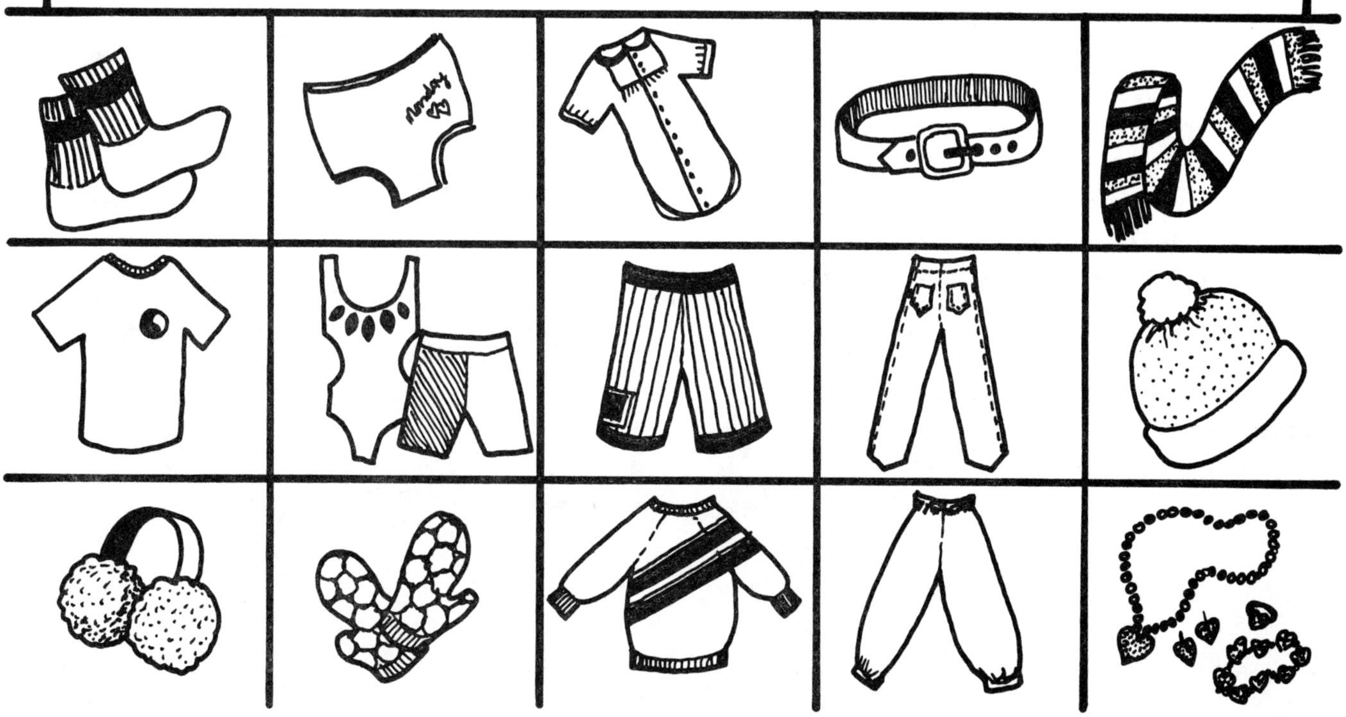

SHOP AND SORT

Here's a fun, hands-on activity that students can experience in three settings—the supermarket, their home, the classroom. It requires that students start with an organized setting (the supermarket where items are located by specific categories), then changes to an unorganized setting (the shopping cart where the items selected are randomly placed), and finally moves to an organized setting (the pantry or refrigerator where items are again organized).

If appropriate, students may go with a parent on a supermarket shopping trip and purchase approximately 20 items. While there, parents should point out the ways food is stocked on the shelves. When they get home, students attempt to organize their refrigerator and pantry by placing like-food items in the same location. Students may work with a parent to see if their refrigerator is very organized, partially organized or unorganized. How can the present way be improved?

After their shopping trip, have a classroom discussion with students about organizing groceries at home and at the market.

In class, reproduce the following "Reorganize the Refrigerator" page for each student. Ask them to place each item on the list in an organized manner in the refrigerator shelves and compartments. They can choose to write the name of the food or draw a picture of it in the space they have selected.

Students should be prepared to explain their system of organization.

Reorganize the Refrigerator

Look at the list of items that you need to store in your refrigerator. Put each item away (by writing or drawing) in an organized system. Decide what you want on each shelf and in each drawer. Which items should go in the freezer? What food do you want in the door? Why?

Food List

jar of applesauce
milk
cheese
hot dogs
mustard
pickles
hot dog rolls
strawberries
jam
eggs
butter
ketchup
bologna
orange juice
diet soda
leftover meatloaf
cream cheese
raisin bread
frozen vegetables
apples
cottage cheese
grapes
lettuce
carrots
leftover spaghetti

Library Line-Up

What would libraries be like without the Dewey Decimal System? If ever a system was needed for organizing, this one has certainly worked well for libraries all over the world.

Create your own library system by listing the main category that each of the following books would be found under. For example, a book on horses would be located under the category of *animals*.

Use only **one word** to describe each category. When you are finished, be ready to participate in a class discussion and name your categories.

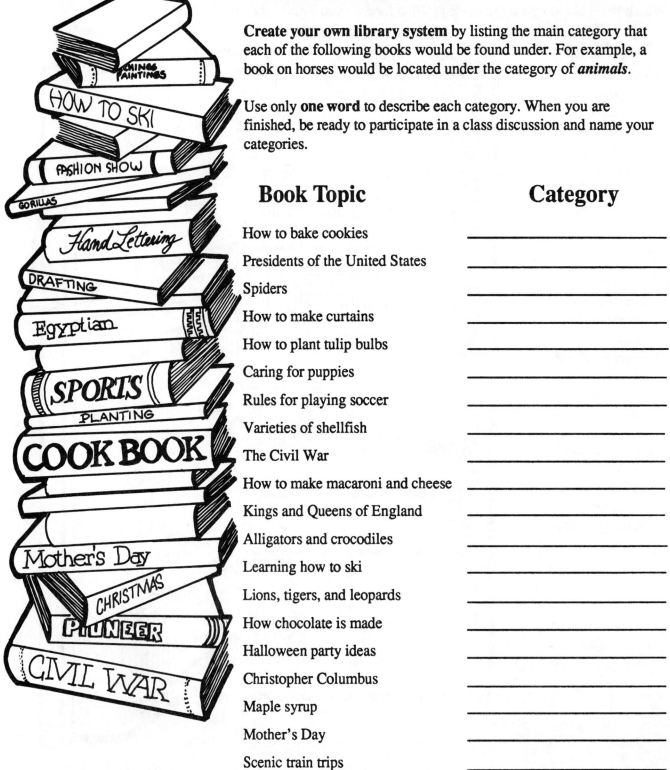

Book Topic	Category
How to bake cookies	_____
Presidents of the United States	_____
Spiders	_____
How to make curtains	_____
How to plant tulip bulbs	_____
Caring for puppies	_____
Rules for playing soccer	_____
Varieties of shellfish	_____
The Civil War	_____
How to make macaroni and cheese	_____
Kings and Queens of England	_____
Alligators and crocodiles	_____
Learning how to ski	_____
Lions, tigers, and leopards	_____
How chocolate is made	_____
Halloween party ideas	_____
Christopher Columbus	_____
Maple syrup	_____
Mother's Day	_____
Scenic train trips	_____

Organization Everywhere!

Without even realizing it, you see organization and systems that work every day in many different places. For instance, when you go into a restaurant with your family and order a meal, how does the waitress or waiter know which table to bring the food order to? There is a system in every restaurant so that tables have specific numbers; the table number is written on the order slip and then the waitress/waiter knows exactly where to bring the order.

Easy systems of organization are all around you! See if you can figure out the organizing system for the following.

Airplane seats are assigned and reserved according to _____.

Food in the supermarket is arranged by _____.

You can find a special service in the "Yellow Pages" by
looking for the service _____.

The post office assigns "Post Office Boxes" for people to
pick up their mail by assigning _____.

Doctors, dentists, hairdressers, etc. keep track of their
appointments by _____.

Clothing in stores is hung on racks to buy according to _____.

Seats at a baseball, football or stadium game are assigned according to_____.

You can find someone's house you've never been to before
because you know _____.

⌐ Be ready to talk about: ─────────────

- How do these organizing systems help to make everyday life easy and manageable?

- How would you know when to watch a special TV program if there was no guide to tell you the day, time and channel?

- What systems does your family use to organize the following: laundry, chores, use of the television?

⌐ Bonus! ─────────

Tell the class about one special organized plan you saw and how it worked.

PHONE BOOK FUN

The most common way of organizing people's telephone numbers is alphabetically **by their last name.** However, if you're not very good at remembering people's last names, this system may not be effective for you.

Here's a list of people and their telephone numbers. It's in no particular order and it's your job to organize it so you can look up telephone numbers easily. Before you start, think about the various ways you can organize this information and what would work best **for you.** Jot your ideas down, explain your organization, and then use the mini phone cards to create your list.

Jot down your ideas here

Mom's friend	Ann Myers	555-1428
My friend	Todd Anderson	555-9980
My friend	Johnny Mills	555-9065
Gardener	Bill Barnes	555-1256
Dance teacher	Laura Smith	555-8871
Dad's office	Larson Printing	555-0086
School	Valley Central	555-7745
Aunt Becky		444-0879
Neighbors	Ruth and Joe Sanders	555-3434
My friend	Rick Lewis	555-2121
Painters	Ken and Jane Ayers	555-6989
Babysitter	Charlene	555-1290
Pizza Delivery	Pete's Pizza	55-PIZZA
Mom's Friend	Joanne Miller	555-9821
Grandma	Marie Milliken	555-3792

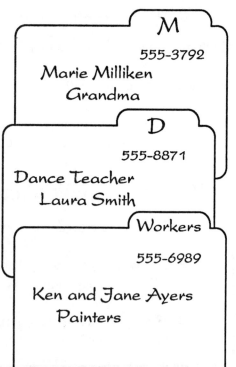

M
555-3792
Marie Milliken
Grandma

D
555-8871
Dance Teacher
Laura Smith

Workers
555-6989
Ken and Jane Ayers
Painters

Prepare your personalized phone index so it is organized, easy-to-read and appealing to look at. Be prepared to hand it in by _____ . Be sure to have your name on the cover!

Two pages per student.

PLAN A PARTY!

*To plan a successful party, it takes all sorts of planning well in advance. As a class project, brainstorm all the planning and organizing that needs to be done **for any party**. Jot down all the ideas on the chalkboard.*

You will then be responsible for organizing a "mock-party." You will need to present the following information in order to complete your assignment.

Use the "Party Planning Page" to organize!

- What is the theme of the party? Plan creatively!

- Compile a guest list that will "work"—blend your list to include outgoing as well as quiet guests. Keep in mind that not everyone who is invited will attend—you may want to "over-invite" so you can be sure of having enough guests for a successful party.

- Decorations add a festive look to any party. Plan a two or three color scheme for your party and plan your decorations and invitations around these colors.

- Create an invitation and submit a completed one as part of the assignment. Show the important information—day, date, time, where it is, what guests may need to bring, etc. Ask guests to RSVP by a specific date so you can plan.

- What will you do for fun? What games will you play? What special things will you need to have ready for the games? Will you need prizes???

- How much will this party cost? Plan your refreshments; then visit the supermarket and write down the costs of **everything** you will need including paper plates, cups, party favors, etc. Submit **"an itemized list"** of planned expenses.

PLANNING PAGE

Party theme: _____

Refreshments to be served: _____

_____

Information to include on the invitation:

Day and date _____ Location _____

Time _____ Given by _____

Special comments _____

Plan a budget. Itemize how much each item will cost and total your expenses. Will you be able to meet your expenses? Remember to include costs for invitations if you plan to "buy" them for your mock-party.

Amount of party budget: _____

Item   **Cost**

_____   _____

_____   _____

_____   _____

_____   _____

_____   _____

_____   _____

_____   _____

_____   _____

                                TOTAL: _____

Pack a Backpack

This backpack has four convenient pockets—three small ones on the front and a large one that closes with a buckle. Think of the things you need to carry to and from school. "Organize" them in your backpack by writing on each pocket what you will put there.

CLASSROOM KICKOFF • © EDUPRESS

> *A note, an award, group or individual recognition…everyone needs a pat on the back for good effort.*
>
> *Here's a variety of easy-to-implement motivational tools from reproducible awards to simple programs.*

Feed Rover—Group motivation

- Enlarge the illustration.

- Color, laminate and tack the dog to a bulletin board.

- On a small table next to the dog, place a bowl of dog biscuits (purchase them at the grocery store) and a second empty bowl.

- When a child has exhibited good behavior or outstanding work, ask him or her to "Feed Rover." (Or any other name the class has selected for the dog.)

- When all the biscuits have been transferred from one bowl to the other, reward the entire class. The reward may consist of a small treat, an extra few minutes of recess or some additional free class time.

Begin again with a full bowl of biscuits.

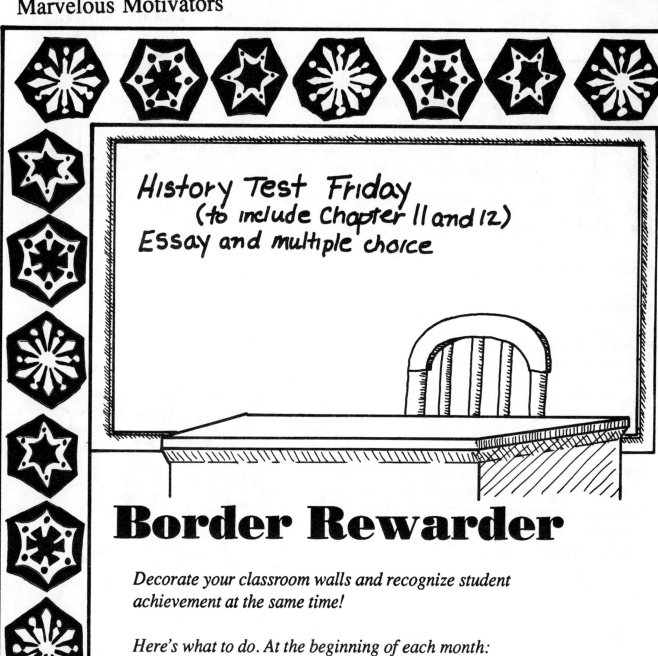

History Test Friday
(to include Chapter 11 and 12)
Essay and multiple choice

Border Rewarder

Decorate your classroom walls and recognize student achievement at the same time!

Here's what to do. At the beginning of each month:

Precut a large supply of seasonal or holiday related seasonal shapes.

Establish a goal the entire class can work toward. You may decide to strive for a neater room, faster cleanup or a day with no tattling! The students can be a part of this decision.

Tack a shape on the wall each time the goal is achieved. Put the shapes in a row and watch the border grow.

Sparkling Clean

Enlist the help of a volunteer to reproduce, cut out and glue glitter to a stack of sparkler awards.

Conduct unannounced checks of desks and work areas. Award **SPARKLERS** to anyone passing the check with "sparkling" colors!

Reward Coupons

Because you offered to help without being asked . . .

. . .you may sit with a friend for a day.

Because you persevered in a very difficult assignment when no one else did...

...you may be first in line for lunch for one week.

Reward special student deeds and positive behavior with **Reward Coupons** that students can "cash in" and collect the specified reward.

Stress to students the importance of keeping their reward coupon to cash in when they want. If it's lost, the reward is not valid!

Reproduce the coupons on the next page on brightly colored paper. Cut them apart and keep them handy to give out for worthwhile efforts.

You may want to create coupons of your own design to suit your classroom needs and goals.

Because you knew all your math facts...

...you may add 10 points to your next math test. (You must attach this certificate to the test!)

Because you cheered up a sad classmate...

...you may choose an art activity for the class.

Because you offered to help without being asked . . .

. . .you may sit with a friend for a day.

Because you are such a careful proofreader...

. . .you may help the teacher prepare a worksheet for the class.

Because you made a new student feel welcome...

...you may help the teacher design and decorate a new bulletin board.

Because you persevered in a very difficult assignment when no one else did...

...you may be first in line for lunch for one week.

Because you respect other people's property...

...you may be the teacher's special assistant for one week.

Because you are so cooperative in class...

...you may be the teacher's special helper for a week.

HELPERS *in the Classroom*

Having classroom helpers is not a new idea. And there's good reason for this traditional classroom procedure! Active participation in class helps children:

Gain *a sense of pride and importance*
Increase *self-esteem*
Practice *giving attention to detail*

Learn *responsibility*
Learn *to follow through on a task*
Feel *are a part of a group*

Here's a list of "Job Assignments" —and their job descriptions–for your students. Some are "old standards" but there may be a few new ones you haven't yet considered!

JOB	DESCRIPTION
Plant Waterer	Keeps green things green!
Animal Feeder	Keeps living things living!
Humor Helper	Maintains a display of comics and cartoons.
Board Washer	Erases the chalkboards at day's end (or when asked).
Flag Salute Leader	Starts the day in a patriotic way.
Calendar Changer	Keeps the class "up to date."
Opening Overseer	Oversees any special opening activities.
Attendance Attendant	Prepares attendance records for the office.
Absentee Assistant	Makes folder of "work missed" for absent students.
Paper Passer	Passes out paper necessary for an assignment
Homework Helper	Notes assignments on the bulletin board.
Conservation Consultant	Keeps recycling center clean, turns off lights etc.
Teacher's Aide	In charge of any extra needs not already covered
Current Event Poster	Posts articles brought in by classmates.
Errand Expert	Takes care of out-of-classroom needs and business.
Message Taker & Sender	Takes notes, attendance to office and other rooms.
Equipment Manager	In charge of handing out & collecting play equipment.
Paper Sorter	Helps sort papers for return.
Chart Charter	In charge of classroom "star" charts, posting results
Coat Closet Coordinator	Keeps forgotten items & leftover lunches to a minimum.
Art Cupboard Attendant	Updates inventory, stocks new items, "tidies" shelves.
Appreciation Aide	Writes thank you notes to visitors, speakers, aides.
Hospitality Helper	Introduces visitors, welcomes new students.
Trash Engineer	Empties trash, oversees floor cleanup.
Line Leader	Leads in, out, to and from!
Sparkle Supervisor	Supervises a clean-looking classroom.
Birthday Rewarder	Makes cards for birthday celebrants/Posts birthdays.
Personnel Director	Someone has to keep track of who has all these jobs!
Key Controller	Unlocks the door to enter, locks the door when leaving.

HELPERS *in the Classroom*

Now that you've chosen the jobs you'd like students to help out with in the classroom, how will you–and the children–keep track of who's doing what, when? Here are some ideas.

HELPING HANDS

Make colorful paper hand cutouts.
Write the job in each hand.
Students create name tags to post underneath.

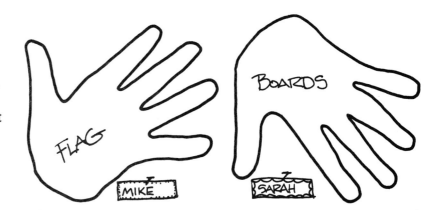

JOB SYMBOLS

Create a colorful student-made symbol for each classroom job.

Art Cupboard Attendant

Janie

Equipment Manager

Billy

Message Taker & Sender

Julie

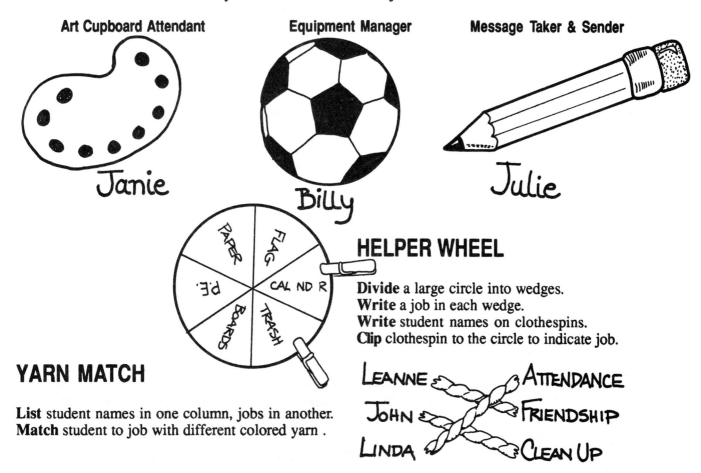

HELPER WHEEL

Divide a large circle into wedges.
Write a job in each wedge.
Write student names on clothespins.
Clip clothespin to the circle to indicate job.

YARN MATCH

List student names in one column, jobs in another.
Match student to job with different colored yarn .

LEANNE — ATTENDANCE
JOHN — FRIENDSHIP
LINDA — CLEAN UP

Marvelous Motivators

Clothespin Competition

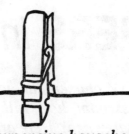

A inexpensive household clothespin can be an effective motivational tool. Keep a big bag of clothespins— brightly painted if you want— hanging on your desk for immediate recognition. Choose from these suggestions.

Cooperative Clothespins

This technique is great if your classroom desks are arranged in clusters of four or more.

Put a *Clothespin Competition* wheel (directions at right) in the center of the desk cluster. Each time the cluster group accomplishes what has been asked— first to clean up, all homework assignments turned in, library books returned on the due date—pin a clothespin to a wedge on the wheel. When every wedge has been "pinned" the group gets a reward.

At this point you can remove the clothespins from **all** the wheels and start over. **Or,** as each group achieves a full wheel, they get the reward, remove their clothespins and start over. The other groups retain what has already been pinned on their wheel and continue .

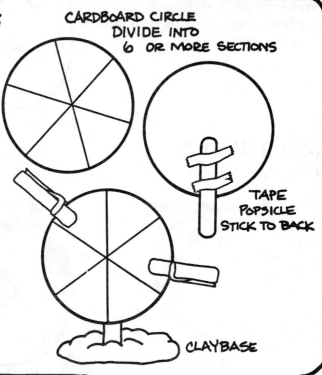

CARDBOARD CIRCLE DIVIDE INTO 6 OR MORE SECTIONS

TAPE POPSICLE STICK TO BACK

CLAY BASE

Pin Me

This is an individual reward system. As you see a student working productively—neat handwriting, completing a task, working cooperatively—reach into your handy bag of clothespins and "pin" it on the child's collar, pocket or sweater.

After a predetermined amount of time—morning before the first recess, for example—students count their clothespins. Reward accordingly:

> the student with the most gets a special treat
> those with one . . . those with two . . .

Return the clothespins to the bag for another time.

Penny Power

Decorate a quart jar with the words "Penny Power".

Children bring in spare pennies to put in the jar. Be sure to discuss with them the need to have permission before any money is brought in. A quick note home (perhaps in your monthly newsletter) can fill the parents in on the plans.

When the jar is full, count the pennies. Use the money to buy special things for the class…a game, a book, a ball, a treat.
You'll not only be motivated but get good practice in counting, budgeting, decision-making and more!

Pick a Card, Any Card

Fill a decorated box with index cards on which a reward has been written.

The rewards can be geared to individuals or to the whole class.

Suggestions:
> Skip a homework assignment
> Have lunch with the teacher
> Game day
> Special treat

Ask the class to help brainstorm different rewards to write on the cards. (With teacher approval, of course!)

Reward behavior, work, citizenship with a trip to the box.

GAME DAY

Skip your Homework Today

Get a FREE Ice Cream at lunch!

A+ for Attendance

If attendance—or tardiness—is a problem in your classroom, here are some quick and easy ways to provide incentives.

IMPORTANT:

When children are ill they **should not** attend school. Let them know that excused absences—those due to sickness and accompanied by a note from an adult—will also be rewarded.

1. Set aside a special, prominent area of the chalkboard or bulletin board to list the names of all students who had perfect attendance or on-time arrivals the previous month. Present these names in a colorful and appealing way. Use colored chalk and bold lettering; Add a border of bright yellow stars. Make students proud to have their names shown.

2. Tell students ahead of time the special treat or activity they will earn for their attendance and promptness efforts. Decide what would motivate **your** class the most…an extra art project?…choosing where to sit in class?…a homemade cupcake? Keep the upcoming reward posted as a motivating reminder.

3. For severe problems, reward offending students on a weekly basis. For students who find it difficult to have a perfect record for a week and then show improvement, provide a 'star chart' or ask the child to be in charge of a class job he favors.

4. Use the special certificates on the following page as "send-home rewards."

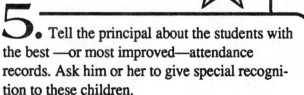

5. Tell the principal about the students with the best —or most improved—attendance records. Ask him or her to give special recognition to these children.

Improved Attendance is something to CROW about!

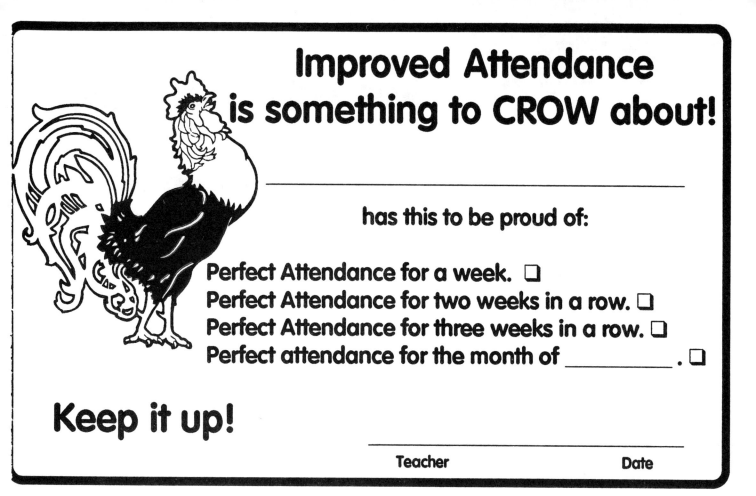

_____

has this to be proud of:

Perfect Attendance for a week. ❑
Perfect Attendance for two weeks in a row. ❑
Perfect Attendance for three weeks in a row. ❑
Perfect attendance for the month of _____ . ❑

Keep it up!

_____
Teacher   **Date**

You're a STAR!

_____

**Our class is better because you were on time every day in the month of_____.
THANKS!**

_____
Teacher   **Date**

for Attendance

_____

can be proud of Perfect Attendance for

_____

I am pleased that you know the importance of being at school every day!

_____
Teacher   Date

Guess who's ON-TIME EVERY-TIME?

It's _____!

for

_____

That's Terrific!

_____
Teacher   Date

for Attendance

_____

can be proud
of perfect attendance
for

_____

I am pleased to see improved attendance and
improved schoolwork!

_____
Teacher   Date

for Attendance

_____

can be proud
of perfect attendance
for

_____

I am pleased to see that you know the importance
of being at school every day!

_____
Teacher   Date

Marvelous Motivators

Clip-Its

Here's an assortment of mini-awards to have on hand.

Reproduce them on colored paper, cut each out on the dotted lines and glue a paper clip to the back.

Then *Clip-It* on a special paper or pocket and watch for smiles!

To:

For:

You're a Star!

Keep up the Good Work!

TO:

FROM:

FOR:

GOOD "EGG" AWARD

Stamp a Spot

Here are three mini-charts for students to use to track individual accomplishments.

● Select a style and reproduce one for each child. Have the children write their name in the indicated place.

● Explain that when they do their best work or exhibit especially good behavior or citizenship they will get a spot stamped on the record sheet.

● When all the "spots" are stamped, they may choose something special to do or receive a simple treat.

NAME

Name

Name

Classroom Notes

A monthly newsletter to parents is a great way to keep them up-to-date with classroom activities. It also keeps the lines of communication open and can potentially answer questions and resolve problems they may have. Hopefully, the newsletter will save you time on the phone, too!

Here's what to do:

• Reproduce a copy of the Classroom Notes form, following, for each month of your school year.

• Several days before the start of the new month, type or write in the information, paste the corresponding clip-art in the box and reproduce a copy for each student. (Better make some extras, too!)

• Be sure to include…vacation dates, assignment due dates, special classroom project needs, suggested books to read, new areas of curriculum content.

Classroom Notes

**Upcoming Events • Dates
to Remember:**

Curriculum focus:

Things to...

...practice

...send in

...read at home

Help needed:

- - - - - - - - - - - - - - - **Clip and send back** - - - - - - - - - -

Yes, I can help with _____ **on** _____

Please call. I have a question about _____

_____

Signed _____

Steps to Student Success

Dear Parents,

Here's a list of suggestions to help ensure your child's success in school and at home. Please use the ones that you believe will work well in **your** home. These are only "suggestions" and are being sent as a cooperative tool for a positive home/school relationship.

LEARNING AIDS

- **Subscribe** to a daily newspaper and keep it available for family discussions on current events. Keep a globe or world map handy to help children locate where events are occurring.

- **Have up-to-date** reference books available such as a dictionary, an atlas and an almanac. These will be used by the adults in your home as well as by the children.

- **Become familiar** with your child's daily or weekly schoolwork by reviewing school papers and tests when they are brought home. Spend a few minutes to see that your child understands his mistakes.

- **Read** as a family venture. Allow children to subscribe to suitable magazines for recreational reading. They will enjoy getting them in the mail!

- **Get acquainted** with your child's textbooks when they are brought home. See what is currently being taught in school and plan family activities around these studies.

WORKING TOGETHER

- **Set aside** family time so that you do your paperwork when children are doing their homework. This will enable your children to see that grownups have "homework" also.

- **Be interested** in your child's day by asking about his friends, afterschool activities, funny things that happened at school or on the school bus, etc. Share **your** day too!

- **Make an attempt** to limit TV watching by viewing programs with your child. Ask questions and discuss the shows you watch together. Share who gets to choose the programs you view together.

- **Make recycling** another family venture. Put each child in charge of a special task.

OTHER TIPS...

■ **Set a positive example** of human values by showing respect, loyalty, trust and responsibility. Children will learn and use these values when they see that you use them.

■ **Praise** your children's efforts as well as their good grades. Praise small efforts as well as the big ones.

■ **Get excited** with your children when **you** learn something new. Children need to see that learning takes place at all ages. Let them see that some things — even for an adult—are difficult to learn.

■ **Know** the activities your child is involved in after school. Know who is in charge. Check to see that the activities are suitable for your child's age and interests.

■ **Inform** the school or teacher of any current family problems that may affect your child's performance and attitude in class. This will enable us to give special attention when it is needed and to be sensitive in needed situations.

ALWAYS HELPFUL!

■ **Establish** an easy-to-read, easily located organizer for each child in your family—a calendar or a chart works well. Show your child's weekly schedule such as tests, reports due, special events, medical appointments, club meetings etc. Show the date and time clearly. Your child will learn to read it and know how to plan for each week.

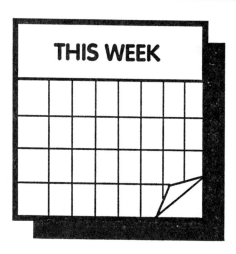

I hope that these suggestions are valuable for your family. Please feel free to share any special successes with me!

Sincerely,

Introducing ... YOUR Child

I'd like to know more about your child, through *your* eyes. The more I know, the better I can tailor an educational and motivational program to fit his or her particular needs.

Please answer the questions and complete the information below. Remember, this is from *your* point of view. I will discuss the same information with your child.

Child's name_____

❧ List *five* words that best describe your child's *character* (competitive, cheerful, perfectionist)

❧ What *motivates* your child?   ❧ What *upsets* your child?

❧ What are your child's out-of-school *interests* and *activities*?

❧ What activities do you *share*? What problems/successes do you have working/playing together?

❧ How would you rate your child's study habits?
Circle one:
1 2 3 4 5 6 7 8 9 10
(awful)   (super)

❧ What *study skills* does your child need to develop? (neatness, timeliness, organization, etc.)   ❧ Which academic subject is your child's best? Worst?

❧ What particular *academic* areas would you like to see stressed?

❧ What *social skills* would you like to see developed?

❧ Are there any *personal or physical problems* I should know (or conference privately) about?

❧ Other comments or concerns?

Parent signature(s)_____

Conference Log

Student _____ Date _____

Attended by _____

Items for Discussion

Parent Evaluation

Recommendations and Goals

Followup Strategies

Signatures

_____

_____

_____

Teacher   Parents, Student

Parents are Partners

"Think through" Your Day!

Use this organizer as a home-school communications tool. Complete the chart as directed then send it home to parents along with the letter (following page). Parents will appreciate any help so that mornings are calm and painless!

■ Have students complete a personalized "checklist" of things they must remember to bring to school on specific days. If Michael goes to a special music class on Tuesday, he needs to remember to bring his violin. If a group of students stays after school on Tuesday and Thursday to practice running, they must bring their running shoes. Is it library day? They must remember to return their book. These are the kinds of reminders that students need to learn to be responsible for—parents need to be brought into this reminder activity so they can do just that...**REMIND** their child without doing it for the child.

■ Ask students to "think through" their day. What special activities does each student have **during** school hours that require something special to be brought from home? List these activities along with related item. What special activities does each student have **after** school hours that requires something special to be brought from home because they attend directly from school? Again, list the activity and the related item.

■ Set up a chart similar to the sample below or students can make their own using this guide. Where will each student keep their reminder chart so it is useful and does the job? Different places will work for different students...

MONDAY		TUESDAY		WEDNESDAY		THURSDAY		FRIDAY	
Special Activity	Need to Bring	Special Activity	Need to Bring	Special Activity	Need to Bring	Special Activity	Need to Bring	Special Activity	Need to Bring

For another activity, have students make another chart listing items *in school that must be taken home.* Work with your students individually—especially with those children that tend to be more forgetful—so they can develop the important skills of organizing, remembering, and being responsible.

Dear Parents,

As a home/school activity, we are working cooperatively to teach our students to "think through" their day. The goal is to instill the lifelong skills of planning ahead, organizing, remembering and being responsible for one's self.

Your child is completing a reminder chart of specific items he or she needs to bring to school on certain days and being taught to prepare for this in an orderly way so it doesn't become a last minute morning rush. Please review it with your child and post it in a conspicuous place. Similarly, I will work in the classroom to be sure children bring home those things they need to have for homework or practice.

Each evening, please work with your child. Ask him or her to "think through" the next school day. What must be brought to school? Refer to the chart. Work with your child to establish a specific place where the items will not be forgotten as he is dashing out the front door (or perhaps it's the back door!)

Again in the morning, ask your child to "Think through your day." Make a "mental visit" to each school subject. Is there any homework that needs to be returned (or hasn't been done)? Are there any things they have forgotten?

Please let me know how I can further work with your child on an individual basis to make these skills work well at home and at school.

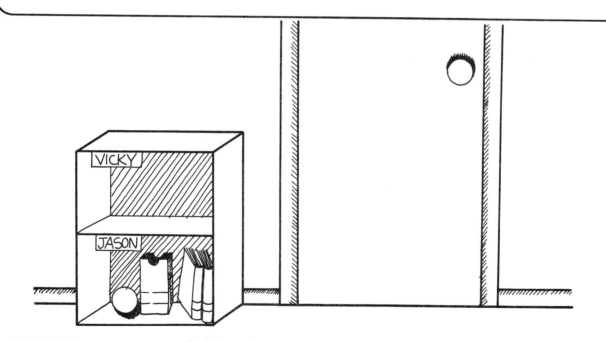

REMEMBER:
"Think through your day."

Motivate with Magazines

Magazines can be great reading motivators! If your students' parents ask for gift or reading suggestions, encourage them to subscribe to magazines for their child.

A complete list of periodicals can be found in the Children's Magazine Guide. This is a subject index to children's magazines. It can be found in the reference section of the public library.

Here are some suggested magazines for children ages 7-12.

Koala Club News
Zoological Society of San Diego
P.O. Box 551
San Diego, CA 92112

Zoobooks
Wildlife Education Association
3590 Kettner Blvd.
San Diego, CA 92101-1139

Highlights for Children
2300 W. 5th Ave.
P.O. Box 269
Columbus, OH 43216-0269

Child Life
Children's Better Health Institute
1100 Waterway Blvd Box 567 B
Indianapolis, IN 46202

Cricket: The Magazine for Children
Carus Corporation
Box 300 315 5th Street
Peru, IL 61354

Cobblestone:History Magazine
Cobblestone Publishing Inc.
20 Grove Street
Peterborough, NH 03458

Humpty Dumpty's Magazine
Children's Better Health Institute
1100 Waterway Blvd—Box 567
Indianapolis, IN 46206

U.S. Kids
Weekly Reader Magazine
P.O. Box 8957
Boulder, CO 80322

WORLD
National Geographic Society
17th and M Streets N.W.
Washington, D.C. 20036

Ranger Rick
National Wildlife Federation
8925 Leesburg Pike
Vienna, VA 22184-0001

3-2-1- Contact
Children's Television Workshop
P.O. Box 50351
Boulder, CO 80322-3051

Plays—Drama Magazine
PLAYS Inc.
120 Boylston St.
Boston, MA 02116

Aide Parade

Parents can be a wonderful resource...if you establish an effective "aide" program in your classroom. Here are some suggestions that will help make your volunteer program one that frees you to work with individuals or smaller groups of children.

Job Possibilities...

Academics:

Flash Card Driller
small group drill and games

Reading Helper
one-on-one reading and story discussion

Spelling Assistant
giving/correcting spelling tests

Library Leader
takes children to library; helps with book selection

Story Secretary
student dictates, secretary writes

Center Supervisor
oversees center activities

Math Referee
officiates math games

Spelling Bee Director
conducts class competition

Dictionary Attendant
helps out during creative writing

Time Tester
administers math-fact timed tests

Organization:

Art Project Preparation
cuts, photocopies, prepares materials

Science Assistant
gathers materials for experiments

Chart Maker
prepares classroom charts

Photocopier
reproduces worksheets

Note Assembler
prepares take-home information

Field Trip Attendant
accompanies class on trips

Party Helper
coordinates party and special day needs

Physical Education:

Referee
oversees sportsmanship and rules

Jump Rope Turner
teaches games

Team Coach
helps with skill and strategy

Motor Development Assistant
works individually with students

Aide Preparation

Meet with all volunteers prior to their work in the classroom.

Establish an "Aide Box" where they will look for daily job direction.

Discuss discipline.

Provide name tags—for students and aides.

Supply a list of all aides and phone numbers. Ask parents to try to find a substitute if they cannot make it to class during their scheduled time.

Student Preparation

Discuss courteous behavior.
Clarify discipline consequences.
Provide cooperation rewards.

Let's Read!

Dear Parents,

We are encouraging children and their families to read at home. Share the joy of reading and enrich your lives through literature.

When you or someone in your family has completed reading a book, either to someone or independently, please complete a reading coupon. A sample is below. More are available in the classroom. Ask your child to bring home a supply. Then sign the coupon and return it to school with your child.

The results will be charted so that everyone can see how much our classroom families enjoy reading. You'll be amazed at the results a few minutes of reading a day can make!

The class will be rewarded for their efforts at school. Please take this opportunity to demonstrate to your child that reading has an important place in the adult world as well as his school life.

Thank you for participating in our **"Let's Read"** enrichment program. We will be encouraging this program throughout the school year and hopefully it will become an important part of your child's daily routine.

Reading Coupon

Student_____

Name of book read_____

Author_____

Read by family member_____ Signed_____

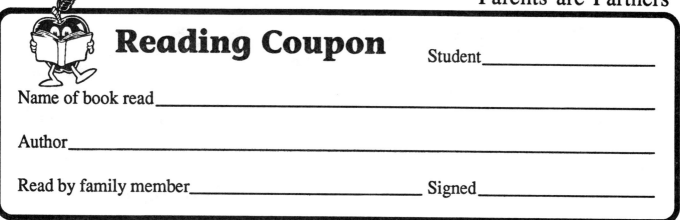

Reading Coupon

Student_____

Name of book read_____

Author_____

Read by family member_____ Signed_____

Reading Coupon

Student_____

Name of book read_____

Author_____

Read by family member_____ Signed_____

Reading Coupon

Student_____

Name of book read_____

Author_____

Read by family member_____ Signed_____

Reading Coupon

Student_____

Name of book read_____

Author_____

Read by family member_____ Signed_____

DECORATING IDEAS

➤ BACKGROUNDS

Turn a drab board into a "jazzy" board with a little imagination, recycling and this helpful page!

Have you tried . . .

- ➤ **felt** for a year-round flannel board
- ➤ **burlap** for a fall harvest scene
- ➤ **aluminum foil** for a chilly winter scene
- ➤ **lace** over pink butcher paper for Valentine's Day
- ➤ **sandpaper** for a beach scene
- ➤ **gift wrap** to coordinate with an upcoming holiday

Or how about a background of . . .

- ➤ newspaper
- ➤ wallpaper samples
- ➤ colorful spatter paint on ordinary butcher paper
- ➤ travel posters

➤ ATTENTION GETTERS

- ➤ butcher paper awning
- ➤ Fiberfill clouds
- ➤ artificial flowers
- ➤ yarn connections
- ➤ crepe paper connections
- ➤ "spot-glued" confetti
- ➤ shiny bows
- ➤ curling ribbon

➤ BORDERS

- ➤ student-made holiday symbols
- ➤ wide, gros-grain ribbon
- ➤ muffin baking cups
- ➤ scalloped paper

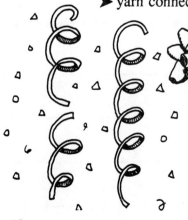

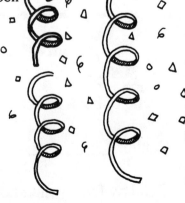

Bright Goals

As a group, brainstorm a list of goals and write them on the chalkboard. Select enough goals to equal the number of students in class.

Reproduce a light bulb for each student and assign them one of the goals to rewrite in the space provided. Collect the bulbs and number the backs consecutively.

Cover a bulletin board with bright yellow paper and add bold white lettering.

Begin with bulb #1 and tack it to the bulletin board. Discuss the goal the students will try to achieve during the day. Evaluate the results before leaving for home. Repeat the process the next day.

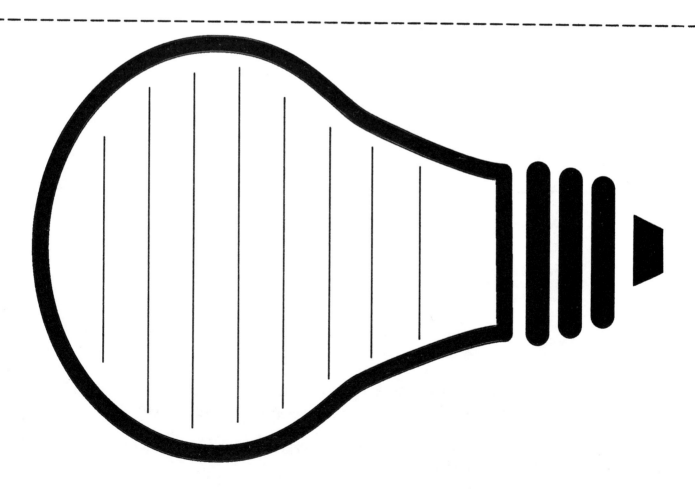

Great Boards from Newspapers

All sections of the newspaper can be used as backing to create some clever, interactive bulletin boards.

Use the **classifieds** ads as display backing for:

>career reports
>
>writing short ads
>
>writing a "personal"—a self-description
>
>finding out what IS in the classifieds

The **classifieds** can also serve as background for a **HELP WANTED** board.

Anytime you need a student to do a special, time-saving job for you, advertise the position on the **HELP WANTED** board. Students can get involved, too, writing short ads to put on the board.

── HELP WANTED ──

WANTED: After-school help filing animal pictures. Needed Tues. or Wed. Ask Miss Smith.

NEED: Helpful person for art mess cleanup Mon. after collages.

FOR SALE: two red unused SNOOPY pencils. Will consider trade. Call Joe.

WANTED: volume #3 of Babysitters' Club. Contact Marcy.

Here are some other lively ideas:

 Back the board with **food ads** for an interactive lesson in math and comparison shopping.

 Use newspaper **headlines** as "springboards" for a creative writing story based on the headline.

 The **sports section** serves as background for biography reports on famous athletes. OR as a math lesson on computing averages for box scores.

 The colorful **Sunday comics** make great backing for student-created cartoon strips or characters.

Book Reports on Display

Students read a book with an **animal** as the center of interest and write a report that includes title, author and short summary.

Then they draw a picture of the animal featured in the book and display it alongside the report.

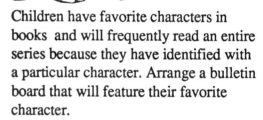

Animals and their Authors

CHARACTER CORNER

Children have favorite characters in books and will frequently read an entire series because they have identified with a particular character. Arrange a bulletin board that will feature their favorite character.

Ask students to write a report about a book in which their favorite character appears, then paint and cut out a colorful picture of the character to display next to their report.

BEST BOOKS

"What's the best book you've ever read?" Ask students this question. Then have them write a short report about the book that, in their mind, answers the question. Ask them to create a book cover, either identical to the actual book or one suited to the book. (See directions for book cover design in START IT IN SEPTEMBER section.) Put the report and the cover on display under the heading **"BEST BOOKS"**.

BIRTHDAY BOARDS

Honor the birthday boys and girls in your class with a special bulletin board. Here are two nifty ideas from which to choose.

Put Another Candle On!

Back the bulletin board in a cheery color.

Create a large birthday cake, complete with frosting.

Reproduce a candle for each student. Ask them to write their name and birthday in the space provided; then color the base and flame.

Each month the birthday celebrants put their candle on the cake.

At the end of the school year, the cake will be "aglow" with one candle for each child in class.

Reproduce one for each student (and anyone else you want to honor)…your principal? school secretary?

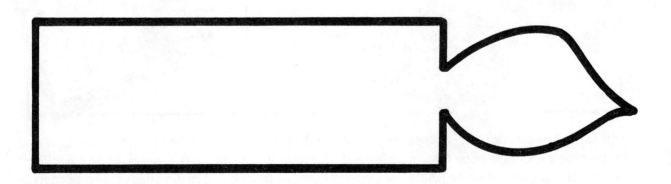

BIRTHDAY BOARDS

Happy Birthday!

Back a bulletin board with birthday-theme gift wrap.

Suspend colorful, shiny ribbon in varying lengths.

Students decorate their own gift (use pattern below) with colorful crayons. Glue on ribbon and a big bow. Fill in the information on the gift tag.

Change the board each month to reflect the birthdays.

Reproduce one for each student (and anyone else you want to honor) . . . your principal? school secretary?

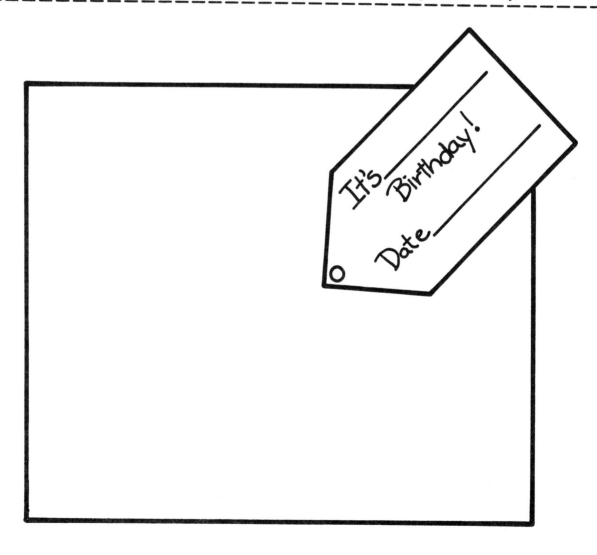

Bulletin Board Library

Create these simple **GOOD WORK** bulletin boards in minutes!

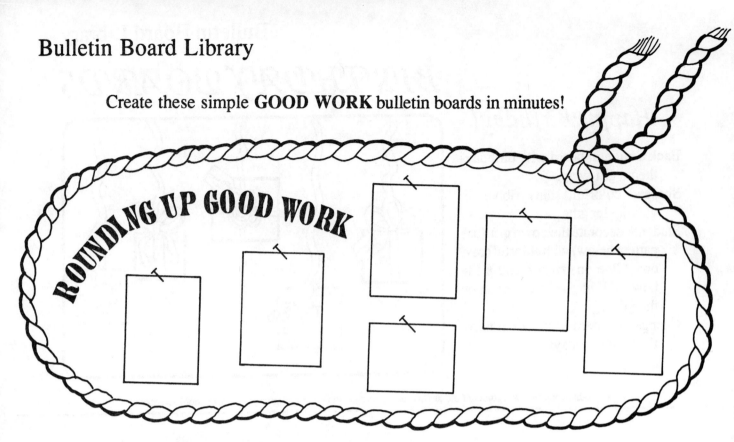

Surround good work with a rope tacked in the shape of a lasso.

Tape cooking utensils—wooden spoon, spatula,
pot holder—around student papers.

CLASSROOM KICKOFF • © EDUPRESS

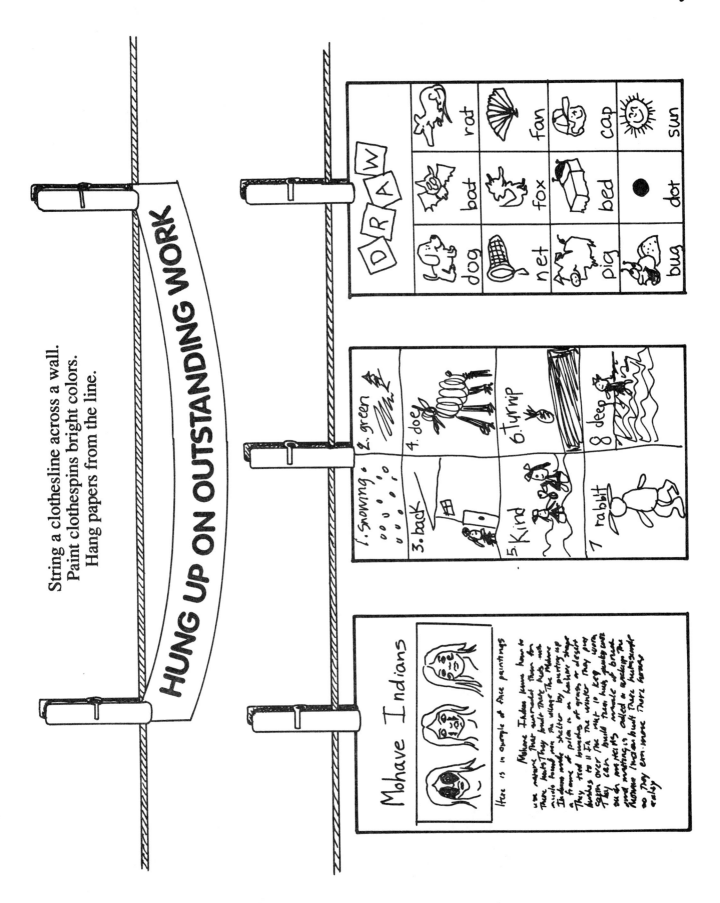

String a clothesline across a wall.
Paint clothespins bright colors.
Hang papers from the line.

HUNG UP ON OUTSTANDING WORK

Year-Round Displays

Here are some displays that start with a basic shape and change to suit all seasons and reasons!

All-Purpose Tree

"Grow" a large dimensional tree in a corner of your classroom. Crumple brown shopping bags and arrange them to form a trunk and branches.

Kids change the leaves according to the season. They color and dress "themselves" under the tree to suit the season's weather.

Or decorate the tree with a holiday theme—ornaments in December, hearts in February.

Ready Teddy

Create a large teddy bear, cut out.

Decorate the bear each month.

• He's ready for school in September holding a book bag and carrying a ruler.

• In October, he's a ghost, November a Pilgrim, December Santa Claus and so on.

• Studying Egypt?…He's a pharoah!

Ask kids to decide on the costume for the next month and to help with the decorating.

Year-Round Displays

School "TIES"

Recycle out-of-style ties collected from willing parents, garage sales or thrift stores. Arrange the ties to create colorful shapes. Add student work for a great display.

Year-Round Displays

DON'T FENCE ME IN!

Recycle a standard curtain rod, any length, with returns at each end.
Attach the rod to the wall for a year-long display.
Cut white paper "pickets" and glue them to the curtain rod to simulate a fence.
Change the scene behind the fence monthly with student-created artwork.

Our Favorite PETS

SCARY Scarecrows

Plant a tree...
...ARBOR DAY

Or try...
• Thanksgiving turkeys
• Spring flower garden
• Chicks in a barnyard

These displays feature the students!

Introducing... **Our School Zoo**

This is a fun way to have children introduce themselves at the start of the school year.

Ask each student to create a self-portrait (face only). Remind them to make their facial features similar to how they look: curly or straight hair, freckles, rosy cheeks and so on. Sign each portrait.

Create scalloped borders and yarn "bars" to cage in the class zoo.

𝕸𝖎𝖗𝖗𝖔𝖗, 𝕸𝖎𝖗𝖗𝖔𝖗... ...𝖔𝖓 𝖙𝖍𝖊 𝖜𝖆𝖑𝖑

Who's the best classroom of all?

Create a mirror by putting aluminum foil in a decorative paper frame.

Surround the mirror with pictures that students have drawn of OTHER classmates.

Caution children that they **must try** to be realistic.

Find out who the real artists are!

Seasonal Sensations

Seasonal shapes lend themselves to sensational interactive displays featuring student writing.

FALL

Cut out a large orange **pumpkin**. Add a green stem.

Cut out a large, white pumpkin seed for each student.

Students list several words on their seed to describe FALL.

WINTER

Create a large **snowman**. Add a top hat, colorful scarf, charcoal eyes, carrot nose and buttoned vest!

Students write a two-line rhyme about WINTER on a large white snowball.

Arrange the snowballs in piles around the snowman.

Seasonal Sensations

SPRING

Greet *SPRING* with a bulletin board listing weather words. Cut out two fluffy white clouds to mount on a blue background

Students cut big, freehand raindrops and write weather words—warm, windy, sunny, hot, humid—on them.

SUMMER

Mouthwatering watermelon creates a tasty display!

Students design red and green slices of watermelon to arrange on a long "picnic table" covered with a plastic checkered tablecloth.

Surround the table with student-drawn pictures that illustrate things they like to do on **SUMMER** days.

Bulletin Board Library
Holiday Ideas

HALLOWEEN

* Green yarn vines
* Student-made jack o'lanterns
* Green paper leaves

JACK O'LANTERN PATCH

BOO-tiful Work!

* White gauze ghosts with
* Black button eyes
* Student papers

"WITCH" book did YOU read?

* Witch with flowing, newspaper hair.
* Halloween-related book reports.

Thanksgiving

Holiday Ideas

🔊 Large, cut-out turkey

🔊 Construction paper feathers

🔊 Students write something they are thankful for on the feather

We're Thankful For . . .

Classroom Pilgrims

🔊 Self-portraits

🔊 Pilgrim hats and collars

A FEAST OF GOOD WORK

🔊 Create a centerpiece: paper candles, candleholder dried flowers

CHRISTMAS

Holiday Ideas

TOP-STARS

☆ Display just the top portion of a Christmas tree.

☆ Put a gold star on the treetop.

☆ Surround the treetop with glittery stars and student work.

Santa's Hat

☆ Create Santa's face, beard, hair.

☆ Students "design" a new hat for Santa.

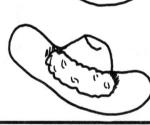

Patchwork Tree

☆ Students each decorate a triangle in holiday colors.

☆ Assemble as shown.

☆ Add a trunk.

Valentine's Day

HEARTS 'n *FLOWERS*

♥ Pink and red scalloped border.

♥ Student-created hearts and flowers.

"Heart"warming Work

♥ Large, decorated heart.

♥ Doily and red paper backing.

♥ Student work.

I Can't RESIST you, Valentine!

♥ Colorful, crayon resist hearts.

Holiday Ideas

Easter

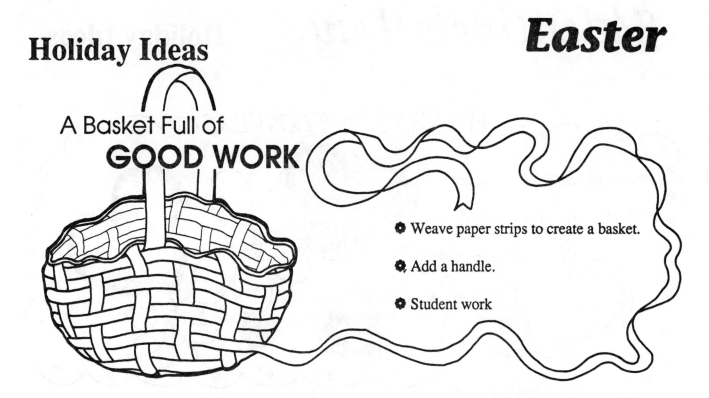

A Basket Full of **GOOD WORK**

- Weave paper strips to create a basket.
- Add a handle.
- Student work

- Artificial grass
- Student-created eggs

EGG GARDEN

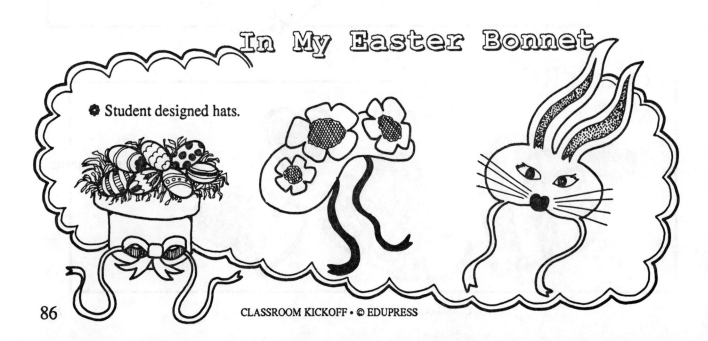

In My Easter Bonnet

- Student designed hats.

DESIGNER DESK TAGS

Desktop name tags, designed by the students, are fun to make and are helpful place markers for visiting parents. Here are several variations to try.

ZIG AND ZAG

Cut a zig-zag shape from colorful construction paper or giftwrap.

Color or cut and paste your name to the shape.

RECYCLERS

Recycle greeting cards for name tags. Cut out pictures, leaving a bottom flap to fold up.

Glue the flap to construction paper.

Use markers to write your name.

SCRAP FUN

Supply paper scraps, trims, scissors and glue. Decorate any shape paper with the cutouts, trim and your name.

HOORAY! for handbooks

Get to know more about each other with "handbooks."

Start by folding plain, white letter-size paper in half.

Trace your hand with crayon on each page. Then color (or cut and paste pictures) and describe something on each page that your "hand" likes to do.

Share your handbook with classmates. Add more pages by folding another sheet of paper in half, sliding it inside and stapling in the center.

"My hand likes to eat hot-fudge sundaes."
"My hand likes to play baseball."
"My hand likes to build sandcastles."

Self Sandwiches

*Students create a **sandwich board** that tells something about themselves. Tell them to keep the information a secret. As a get-acquainted activity, put on the sandwich boards and interview each other. Can they discover the information their classmates were trying to share?*

Making a sandwich board is simple:

1. Cut two identical circles, large enough to cover a student's chest.

2. Connect the circles with strips of construction paper long enough to fit over the shoulders.

3. Decorate both circles.

Here are some ideas to share with students to get them started:.

You have a music lesson or soccer practice at a certain time each week.
> *Draw a large, colorful clock. Put the hands on your lesson or practice time.*

You like to collect butterflies.
> *Cover your circle with pictures of colorful butterflies.*

You are an "ice cream fanatic"!
> *Paint a yummy ice cream cone on your sandwich board .*

Information about outer space fascinates you.
> *Turn your circle into a map of the solar system.*

Your family is very large!
> *Paste pictures of family members all over the sandwich circle.*

NAME BANNER

Here's an easy, colorful addition to your classroom.
Plus, kids will enjoy seeing their name suspended in mid-air!

DIRECTIONS

Provide construction paper, butcher paper, scissors, glue, crayons and markers.

Cut, color and paste to create an individualized name banner. It can be any shape and the name can be written in any direction.

The only requirements are that the banner must fold in half for hanging and that both sides are decorated. (Unless the banner is going to hang along a wall.)

To create the final effect, hang the completed banners over a clothesline and suspend it across your classroom!

Designer Buses

Tired of those plain yellow schoolbuses you see around town? Use your imagination and design a new paint job for the schoolbuses in your town.

Here's What to Do:

Cut out a large bus shape from white construction or butcher paper. Use temperas to paint your bold new design!

Art Potluck

Hopefully you stocked your art cupboard as was suggested on page 14 in the LET'S GET ORGANIZED section of this book. You'll be happy if you did because here are loads of suggestions of how to use some of that unusual "stuff" you collected! And if you haven't stocked that art cupboard yet, it's never too late.

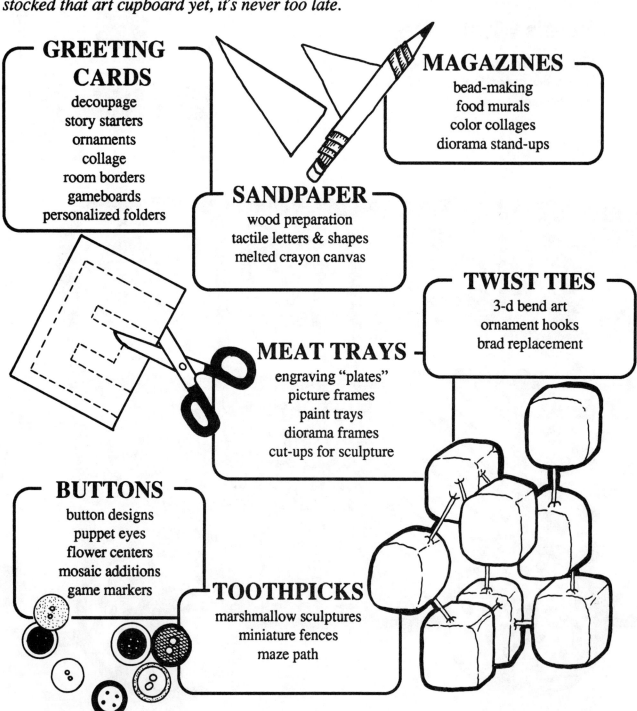

GREETING CARDS
decoupage
story starters
ornaments
collage
room borders
gameboards
personalized folders

MAGAZINES
bead-making
food murals
color collages
diorama stand-ups

SANDPAPER
wood preparation
tactile letters & shapes
melted crayon canvas

TWIST TIES
3-d bend art
ornament hooks
brad replacement

MEAT TRAYS
engraving "plates"
picture frames
paint trays
diorama frames
cut-ups for sculpture

BUTTONS
button designs
puppet eyes
flower centers
mosaic additions
game markers

TOOTHPICKS
marshmallow sculptures
miniature fences
maze path

ROPE
bulletin board border
western art
ceiling hangers
coiled coasters

WIRE HANGERS
yarn-covered gift
bubble-blower frame
embroidery hoop
mobile base
frame for hanging butterflies

ALUMINUM FOIL
paint "canvas"
freeform sculptures
torn "glitter" bits

FELT
bookmarks
flannel board cut-outs
puppets
ornaments
costume decoration
headbands

POP-TOP TABS
picture hangers
clay carver
dough carver
animal eyes
random designs

RAFFIA
monster hair
Indian headdress
African mask trim
scarecrow stuffing

PAPER TUBES
napkin rings
puppets
pencil holders

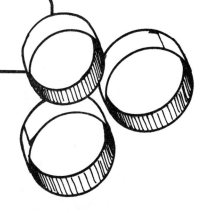

BURLAP
bulletin board backing
paint canvas
fringed banner
Indian costume
gingerbread men

BROWN LUNCH BAGS
holiday treat bags
hand puppet
stuffed turkey centerpiece

GIANT Group Art

This easy art project can be changed and adapted to fit any holiday, season or subject.

On butcher paper, use marker to draw a large, bold outline of an object.

Cut out the shape. Divide and cut the shape into a section for each person in the group.

Students decorate a section in their choice of color and design.

Reassemble the object and create a bulletin board display.

Try the project with these objects:

Fall leaf
Halloween pumpkin
Christmas stocking
Valentine heart
Easter egg

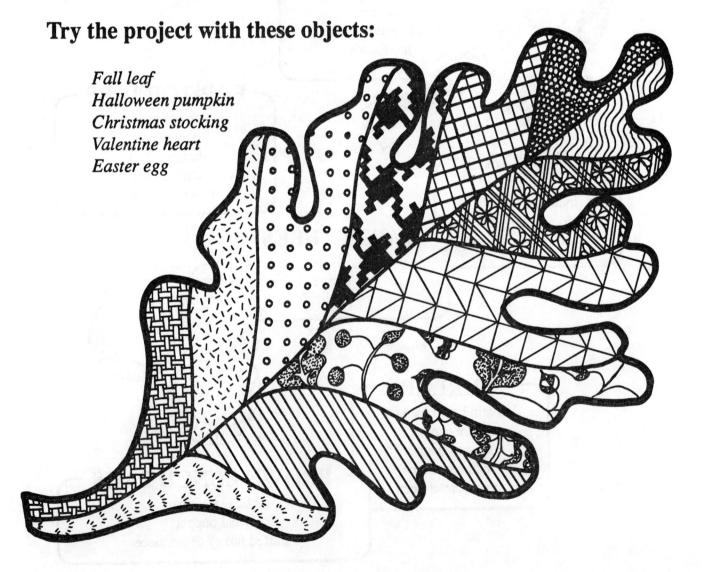

Stand-Ups and Hang-Ups

Materials:

2 pieces construction paper, identical in size
scissors
glue
crayons

Directions:

1. Fold the construction paper together in half, lengthwise.

2. With the paper still folded, cut several zig-zag or curving lines from the fold, out toward the edge of the paper then back to the fold again.

3. Open the papers, separate and decorate both sides with crayon.

4. Run a line of glue along the fold. Glue the two sheets of paper together. Allow to dry.

5. When dry, open and refold in opposite directions. Stand up on a desk or hang-up from the ceiling.

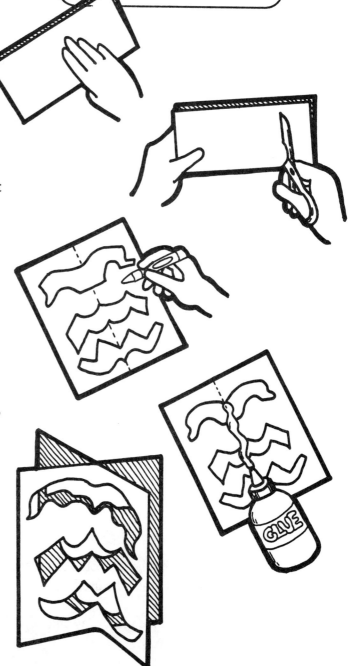

TEAR IT UP

*Two minutes to prepare and two minutes to clean up—
—but lots of time to create and enjoy.
That's what makes this project so great!*

PREPARATION:

- one large sheet construction paper per student in assorted colors.
- glue or paste

DIRECTIONS:

- Tear a large, freeform shape from the construction paper. The shape should require about one-half to two-thirds of the paper.

- Put the remaining scraps in a pile with scraps from the other students at your table.

- Tear shapes from the remaining scraps and glue them, overlapping and creating thickness, on the original shape.

Tell students that when the project is complete there should only be a bottle of glue or jar of paste left...all scraps should be used.

Clean up is easy...put the glue away and wipe the tables.

String Thing

Get to know more about each other. Hang these "string things" over students' desks or on a bulletin board under their names.

Materials needed:

length of yarn for each student
glue
construction paper
magazines
paper hole punch
scissors
crayons

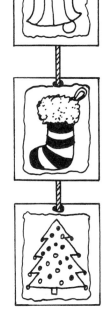

Directions:

Illustrate or cut out and mount magazine pictures that show things you like...food, sports, hobbies, clothes etc.

Punch a hole in the top of each picture.

String yarn through at intervals. (See illustration)

Attach each picture securely to yarn with glue or staple.

Planning Ahead

Adapt this idea to any holiday. String up holiday symbols. For example:

Christmas—stocking, elf, tree, ornament
Halloween—witch, mask, ghost, pumpkin

CEILING SPECIALTIES

> *Enliven your classroom "sky" with these easy-to-make mobiles. Students can make these in their free time. Say "STOP" when the ceiling looks special! Change the colors to suit the holiday or season.*

▼ Provide scissors and a variety of colored construction paper circles, squares and triangles.

▼ Have a practice session with the class first. Show them how to sketch and then cut along dotted lines within each shape.

▼ Hang the finished shape with a contrasting color of yarn.

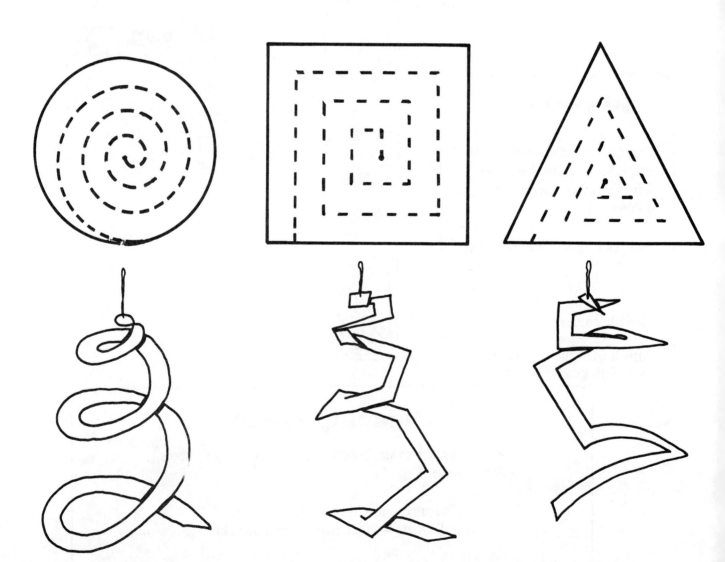

CEILING SPECIALTIES

> *These shapes involove a more advanced procedure—cutting and folding.*
> *Follow the diagrams to make colorful . . .*

Each shape begins with a square.
The folding and cutting techniqes are slightly different.

4-CORNERED STARS

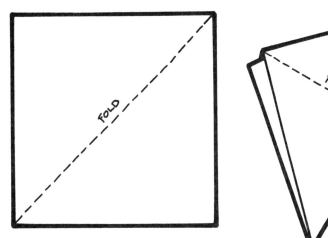
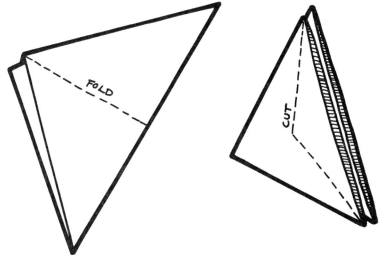

SNOWFLAKES

▼ To make a snowflake, first make a star. Keep the paper folded.
▼ Cut designs along each edge.

Off to a Good Start

The first fifteen minutes of each school day are extremely busy ones for every teacher. You have a lot of details to attend to—roll call, lunch count, collecting notes—to name a few.

These opening moments can be valuable ones, filled with lots of independent learning. Take the time to establish some opening routines and activities that can be ongoing and varied throughout the year.

Here are some suggestions to get things off to a good start.

Establish a weekly schedule for your opening routine. Post a schedule for students to follow.

For example:
The routine may change daily.

Monday—journal entries
Tuesday—boxed games
Wednesday—word of the day
Thursday—group graph
Friday—review skill

Or, the routine may be the same for a week or every morning.

Flag salute
Opening song
Journal observations
Independent reading

Whatever the routine, it should be clear, need no further instruction and allow you, the teacher, to conduct your business within as little time and with as few interruptions as possible.

Set the tone for a successful day…consider the ideas on the following pages…
JUST FOR OPENERS!

ACTION OPENING

The morning buzzer rings to signal the start of the school day. The children eagerly line up at the classroom door. Surprise ! There's an ACTION SIGN on the doorway! This is how they are to enter the room!

Alert them to the possibility of the sign beforehand. Discuss safety rules. If they are to enter the room walking backwards, for instance, talk about looking over their shoulder for other students and to avoid bumping into anyone else.

Here are some *ACTION* SIGN movements to try.

tiptoe

hop on one foot

slow motion

baby steps

elephant walk

jump

march

slow spin

skip

crawl

backward

knees high

stomp

two steps forward, one back

Message Center

> *Get the morning started without saying a word!*

Establish a **MESSAGE CENTER** for your students. Train them to check here each morning for duties, errands and tasks other than the ones already assigned.

For **younger students,** keep the message simple. This provides an opportunity for them to practice their beginning reading skills.

Beforehand, practice the words they might find on the message board. Use illustrations and other visual props, if necessary, to help them understand the message.

MESSAGES

Bill—feed the fish

Ann—pass out lined paper

Older students can get some practice building their vocabulary.

Laurie—**Distribute** the social studies textbooks.
Kevin—**Confirm** the reservation for the auditorium at 2:00 p.m. today.

Everyone—begin reading chapter 5 in your science book.

MESSAGES

If students do not see a message that applies to them, they carry on with their previously established morning routine.

Yellow Brick Road

Are your students tired of sitting in the same old spot every morning when they come in?
Surprise them once in a while with a change of scenery!

Cut yellow, constructon paper "bricks" (rectangles). Or, for a more authentic feeling, paint some real bricks a bright lemon yellow and use them as a border.

Lay the bricks on the floor, from the entry door, leading to a location in the classroom—a center, a general meeting spot, in front of the aquarium or the classroom library, for example. Train the first person in line to FOLLOW THE YELLOW BRICK ROAD and lead the rest of the class to a new destination.

Have instructions waiting there—or meet them there yourself —and read a story, tell a tale, sing a song or try something different for opening.

You can be sure that all eyes will be focused on the floor when the classroom door opens first thing in the morning!

STUMPERS

Get those brains in motion and start the day with a STUMPER.

Students get out paper and pencil and try to come up with as many responses as requested.

Adapt the STUMPER to your students' ability level. Spelling doesn't count—unless this is to be a dictionary activity, too. Answers may vary.

Ask students to participate in creating STUMPERS for the class. (They should know the answers!)

Here are some **STUMPERS** to get you started:

Name eight (8) body parts containing three (3) letters.

leg, toe, hip, lip, rib, ear, arm, eye

Name seven (7) dwarfs.

Sleepy, Sneezy, Doc, Dopey, Grumpy, Happy, Bashful

List six (6) shades of red.

scarlet, burgundy, raspberry, maroon, cardinal, magenta

Name six (6) fruits that begin with the letter **P**.

plum, pineapple, pear, peach, papaya, persimmon

Name five (5) vegetables that begin with the letter **C**.

carrot, cucumber, celery, cabbage, cauliflower

Name five (5) fairy tales.

Cinderella, Sleeping Beauty, Rapunzel, Hansel and Gretel, Jack and the Beanstalk.

ALPHA— Bits and Bites

Alphabetizing is a skill that makes an easy, excellent opener any morning!

As children enter in the morning have them check the **OPENER** space set aside on your chalkboard. If they see the code **"ABC"** they will know to get out paper and pencil and alphabetize what is there.

Check responses immediately after opening business is finished or during reading lessons.

The degree of difficulty can be increased according to the learning level of your students. Look at the sample "boards" for some ideas.

As students improve their alphabetizing skills, add thinking skills to the effort. Have them create their **own** list of words to alphabetize. For example:

ABC	ABC	ABC
6 rhyming words	8 vegetables	10 action words

Their lists may look something like this:

4 rhyming words— brown, clown, drown, frown

8 vegetables—artichoke, beans, beet, cabbage, carrot, lettuce, peas, squash

10 action words—crawl, dive, hop, jump, leap, run, skip, spin, sprint, throw

Weekend Wrapup

> This is a fun word association activity the children will look forward to playing on Monday morning. It also gives them a chance to relive their weekend activities.

Here's what to do:

Ask each child to say two words that remind them of something they did that weekend. Don't ask why they chose those words. Write all the word pairs and the name of the student who said them on the chalkboard.

After several students have taken a turn, ask other students to create a possible activity from each word pair.

For example, if the word pair "John" says is *football* and *hotdog* the player might say "John spent the weekend playing football with a hotdog."

Then ask John to tell what the words really mean. He may have gone to a football game and eaten a hotdog. Or, the words may not be related at all. He may have gone to a party and taken a football as a gift. Then perhaps his family had a barbeque beachparty the following night.

Get ready for some laughs and memory sharing that will start your week out on a happy note!

Easy Opening Activities

Word of the Day

Create a "Word of the Day" box on the chalkboard. When students see a word there they do one or more of the following activities:

Look up the word in a dictionary.
Write the meaning of the word in their "Personal Dictionary". (See pages 132-133.)
Write a sentence using the word.
Illustrate the word.
Find the word in a newspaper or magazine and circle it.
Check a thesaurus and find two synonyms.

Let's Exercise

Some quiet stretching and bending exercises, led by a student helper, gets those muscles and brain cells ready to go! With the help of your students, create a morning exercise routine for the leader to follow. The leader can add some simple movements if he or she wants.

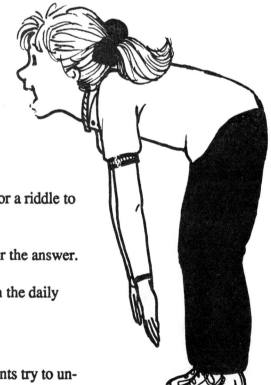

Questions and Riddles

On the chalkboard, write a question to be answered or a riddle to be solved.

Students can check reference or reading materials for the answer.

Be sure to discuss the answer before continuing with the daily schedule or at some time during the day's activities.

Word Scrambles

Scramble a word or phrase on the chalkboard. Students try to unscramble it.

They can also use their class list to unscramble student names as a "getting to know your classmates" activity.

For a Change...

Add variety to routine school schedules by starting your day in a different way. Here are some suggestions to get going with...

Sing a Song
It can be a seasonal, patriotic or holiday song.

Set the Mood
Play morning music for quiet reading time. Ask students to come prepared with a good book.

Read Aloud
Read to your class from a favorite book.

Read a Special Poem
Try a humorous poem or a descriptive one or a series of poems by a favorite author.

"Hear" a Book
Check out a book tape from the library. Play ten minutes of it each morning.

TV Talk
Allow students to discuss what they watched on television the night before.

Start with Art!
Have an early-morning art activity instead of the traditional midday or end of day lesson.

Let's Laugh!
Ask children the day before to come in with a joke or riddle to share.

For a Change...

Have a Snack

Start with a snack! What a nice surprise to give a light munch as a morning treat. Raisins, apple or orange slices, a mini-cup of juice and a slice of cheese are tasty treats.

Or you might sample a food associated with a unit you are studying.

Say It in Spanish

Learn to say phrases and sentences in other languages. Perhaps students can supply the lesson!

Be a Quiz Kid

One child is the quiz kid. Students have three minutes to ask the quiz kid questions about a topic of the quiz kid's choice.

Create a Color Picture

Write a combination of two or more colors on the chalkboard.

Students pull out crayons and plain paper and create a design or picture using only those colors.

Clean It Up

Students spend five SILENT minutes cleaning, organizing and arranging their desks.

Review a Film

Show a short documentary or informational film. A planned lesson, based on the film, may follow.

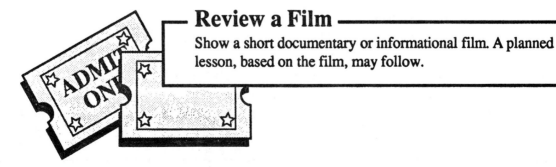

Just Say the Word!

This brief verbal activity is intended to encourage quick thinking by students. Give a category or clue no more than 30 seconds before students are to begin responding.

As your students enter the room, they are required to give a one-word answer in response to a category or clue you have given. As each child tells you his word, it should not be heard by other students who haven't yet responded. As children whisper or give their soft-spoken response to you, they may enter the room if their answer fits the category. If not, students may try again.

Other incentives: students who respond correctly on the first try may write their name on the board, have special free time, etc.

Base your categories or clues on your grade level as well as student abilities. Some suggestions to get you going:

- Name a breakfast food.
- Name a jungle animal.
- Name a kind of bread.
- Name a country in the news.

- Name a flower **other than** a rose or a daisy.
- Name a food that must be kept in the refrigerator.
- Name a foreign language **other than** French or Spanish.
- Name a television show that is on Monday evenings.

WET WRITING

This handwriting practice activity is popular with students of all ages. Use it to have children practice correct letter formation when they are learning manuscript in the lower grades or as they learn cursive in the middle grades.

Prepare the chalkboard with the letter or letters you wish to have students practice. Provide guide lines for letters. Using different bright-colored chalk, write several letters for a group of students to trace.

Students come to the chalkboard and use their finger, which has been dipped into a cup of water placed on the chalkboard ledge, to trace the letters. As each traced letter dries, the water 'sets' the colored chalk onto the board (but can be washed off.)

This activity provides a different type of kinesthetic approach to letter formation.

Try **these** other approaches too:

• **write** letters in a box filled with sand or cornmeal

• **write** letters in the air.

• **write** letters on velvet or sandpaper.

First Day Frenzy Fighters

Welcome!

Write a welcome letter to each student in your class. With it, attach a "special pencil". Students will enjoy reading the letters and will be ready to go to work with a newly sharpened pencil!

Picture This

Take photographs of your students starting on the first day. Display the photos on a bulletin board. Studets will enjoy looking at the ways they've changed.

Divide the pictures at the end of the year so that each student has some to remember his class by.

Show and Tell

There are certain supplies you may want students to supply on their own. Set up a display table so they can visually see what it is you are requesting.

This should resolve some potential memory problems!

Instant Motivator

Involve students in an art activity that you will use as part of a bulletin board display.

They will look forward to the next day when they will see the exciting and colorful results of their efforts on display

Cleaning Encouragement

◆**AWARD** bonus points for unrequested cleanup volunteers.

◆**ASK** a student to name a number. It might be the day's date, their age or any number they think of. That becomes the number of things each student must pick up from the floor.

◆**CONDUCT** surprise desk checks. Award small prizes.

◆**PROVIDE** table-top awards for clean desk tops.

◆**USE** a stopwatch to time cleanup. Record the time and save it in a special area on the chalkboard. The class tries to its time each day.

◆**APPOINT** classroom inspectors. It's their job to check cleaning progress and assign others to take care of unfinished business.

◆**BUY** a small stuffed animal. Ask students to help you name it.
For example:

a lion named **King Clean**
a bear named **George the Janitor**
a puppy named **Sniffin'**... (around for
      something clean!)

After the children leave for the day, set the animal on the desk of a student who did an extra-special clean up job that day. In the morning, the children will be excited to see who gets to keep the stuffed animal for the day. (Older students' enjoy this, too!)

◆**REWARD** individual cleaning contributions with **CLEAN TICKETS** that can be cashed in for small prizes such as peanuts, stickers and small boxes of raisins.

Classroom Management

I'm Done!

Tired of hearing those words from your students? Here's a solution.

Provide a different color folder for each subject. Set the folders on a shelf under a sign that says "When you're done…" Students know just where to put completed papers.

Pick a Stick

Write each student's name on a popsicle stick. Store the sticks in a clean, decorated coffee can. Need a helper for a special errand? a leader for a game? someone to write on the blackboard? Pick a stick from the can!

Stand Up and Be Counted

Here's a way to find out who has completed an assignment or project. Collect all papers, ask students to stand when their name is called. Read through the papers. Those students still seated have not completed the work.

Easy Attendance

Tape a library pocket for each student on a bulletin board.

Keep a can of brightly painted popsicle sticks nearby. When students arrive in the morning, they put a stick in their pocket. Attendance taker can tell at a glance who is absent.

The same system can be used for lunch buyers. Color code a popsicle stick for "buyers" who will put the stick in their pocket in the morning.

A monitor empties the pockets before leaving school.

Classroom Management

Put It Here

End the time wasted answering the question "What do I do with this?" On a special table, set trays or boxes clearly labeled:

> Things to be returned
> Notes for my teacher
> Homework

Students place communication and notes in these trays for you to review at your convenience.

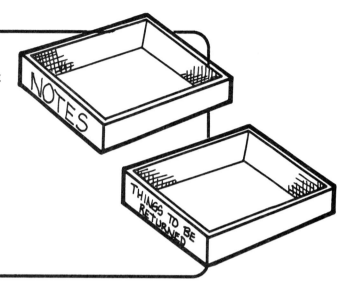

No Name

Tell students that papers with no name on them will be placed in a box labeled

"PAPERS NEEDING A HOME"

It will be their responsibility to look there for assignments they have not received credit for because they forgot to write their name on it.

Homework Helper

Give student memories a boost with an easy *homework reminder system.*

List subject areas across a bulletin board or other display area. Under each subject place a suction cup hook. Hang a colored card with a hole punched in it on the hook under the subject.

Students can tell, at a glance, what areas they have assignments in. If they don't know what the assignment is in a particular subject they can ask a fellow classmate for the information.

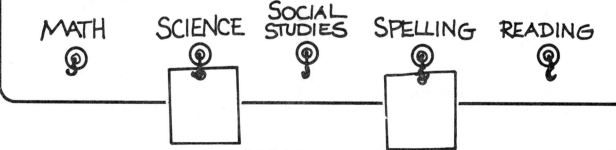

Bulletin Board Management

Storage Ideas

✳ Make large **portfolios** from butcher paper or buy portfolios at an artists' supply store. Label by month, subject area or designation of your choice.

✳ Roll up large graphics and insert them into long, **cardboard tubes** (from gift wrap, for instance).

✳ Hang with **clothespins on hangers** in a closet. Cover with plastic dry cleaning covers.

✳ Roll up and slide through **plastic six-pack rings**.

✳ Put smaller pieces and lettering in **clear plastic storage bags.**

✳ Buy a **zippered notebook pencil holder** for each month or bulletin board. Keep them in a notebook on your desk.

✳ **Laminate** EVERYTHING!

Inexpensive Ideas

Recycle greeting cards

✳ Use as **border trim.**
✳ Create a **story starter** or student **sketching** board.
✳ Increase size with an **opaque projector.** Color or paint.
✳ **Cut out characters** for bulletin board "puppets" or accents.

Calendar Markers

✳ Ask students to create calendar markers using **scraps from the art cupboard.** The ones they make will be wonderful additions to any calendar!

Lettering

✳ Cut word and letters from **magazines.**
✳ Use a **template** to trace and cut letters from various kinds of paper and material.

Tips from Teachers

Post this list—or duplicate a copy for each student to have at his fingertips. When work is completed, students can select from this list of suggestions to use their time effectively.

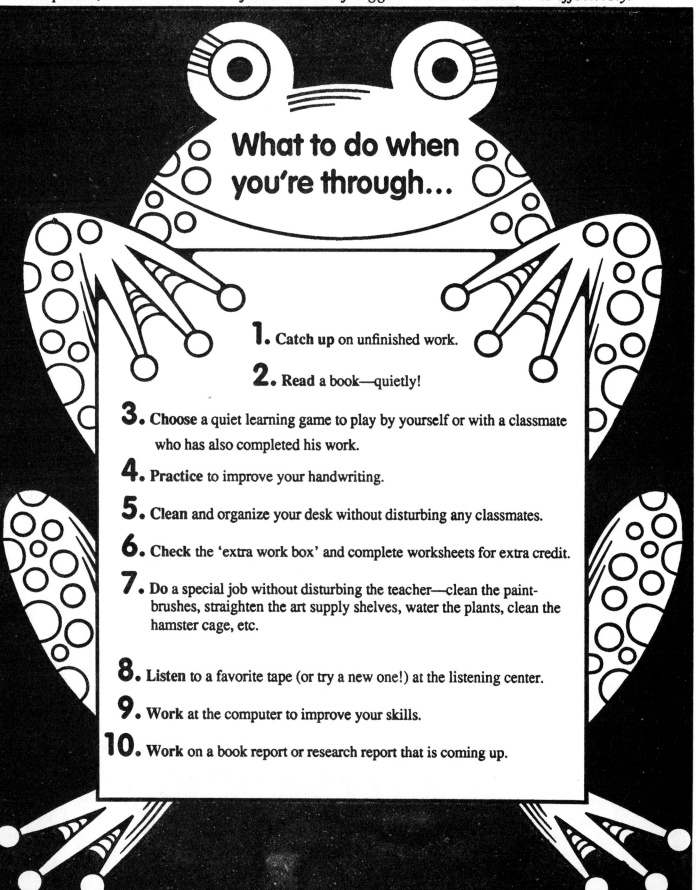

What to do when you're through...

1. **Catch up** on unfinished work.

2. **Read** a book—quietly!

3. **Choose** a quiet learning game to play by yourself or with a classmate who has also completed his work.

4. **Practice** to improve your handwriting.

5. **Clean** and organize your desk without disturbing any classmates.

6. **Check** the 'extra work box' and complete worksheets for extra credit.

7. **Do** a special job without disturbing the teacher—clean the paintbrushes, straighten the art supply shelves, water the plants, clean the hamster cage, etc.

8. **Listen** to a favorite tape (or try a new one!) at the listening center.

9. **Work** at the computer to improve your skills.

10. **Work** on a book report or research report that is coming up.

Storage Ideas

It seems like there's never enough cupboards, shelves, bins or boxes to stash all the things you need to run your classroom. Read through these storage ideas that teachers have shared for some nifty ways to organize clutter in your classroom.

See-through Storage

Clear plastic bins make wonderful storage containers. They stack easily and you can see, at a glance, what is in them.

In This Drawer . . .

Check your local builders' supply store for a multi-drawer container (usually plastic) used to hold miscellaneous hardware items such as spare nuts and bolts. The drawers are various sizes . . . just perfect for buttons, sequins, beads and other unusual trims you keep on hand for dazzling art projects.

Berry Nice Storage

Berry baskets make convenient bins for crayons or markers. They stack together (if not too full) and make clean up easier.

Tube Rolls

Save those long inner-tubes from gift wrap for storing classroom charts or bulletin boards. The tubes don't take up much room and it's practically guaranteed that corners won't wind up bent or frayed. Several tubes may be held together with a rubber band and stacked in a shelf. Be sure to label the tube's contents before putting it away.

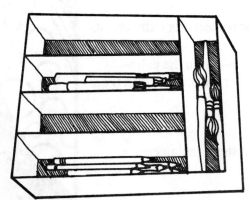

Classroom "Utensils"

Silverware trays hold a different kind of utensil in your class cupboard. Paint brushes and colored pencils fill the sections nicely.

Storage Ideas

Tub Tricks

You can never have too many margarine and whipped topping tubs on hand for instant storage:

Their air-tight seal is perfect for prolonging the life of tempera paints. And as an added bonus, you don't have to try to get the excess paint back in that tiny mouth on the tempera bottle.

Assorted beans and macaroni will never wind up in a pile on your floor should the container accidentally get knocked over.

Eliminate tangles by storing string or yarn in a tub. Cut a small hole in the lid and thread the yarn through. Then just pull and cut off the amount you need.

Handy Totes

Six -pack bottle holders convert easily to tempera paint carriers. When it's paint mixing time, just grab the carrier by the handle and easily transport six paint bottles to your art area.

Gallon Recyclers

Cut the top portions off gallon-sized plastic milk containers for oversized storage.

Expanded File Boxes

Computer disk storage files convert into a maxi-file for your desktop. Cut index cards to fit and divide information into each section. These files certainly hold more than the average recipe file box!

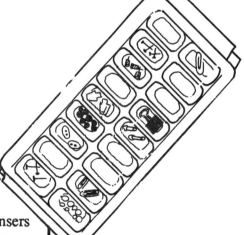

Tall Storage

Oatmeal cartons and tall chip dispensers make great storage for paint brushes, rulers and other tall, top-heavy items.

Storage Cubes

Ice cube trays also make handy dividers for an assortment of hard-to-keep-track-of mini supplies.

And don't forget the old standards . . .

egg cartons, small buckets, t.v. dinner trays, zip-top bags, bathroom tissue dispensers, and boxes of all sizes

Here's My Handwriting!

✎ During the first week of school, select a simple sentence or a short paragraph depending on students' ability. Ask each student to copy this selection **in his best handwriting**. Include student's name and the month.

✎ During the first week of each school month students rewrite the same selection.

✎ At the end of the school year, children arrange the samples into booklets starting with the September sample and ending with the June sample.

✎ Design a cover and present this as a gift to parents.

✎ Both parents and students will delight in seeing how their handwriting progressed and improved throughout the year.

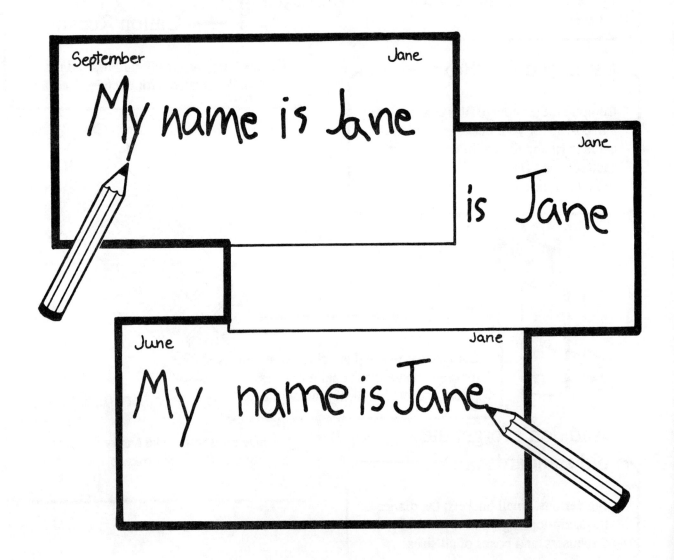

Just the Right

Academic Growth isn't all you can chart this school year!

HEIGHT

> *Measure your students' height during the first month of school and again during the last month—or any time in between. Then when you say "I think you've grown like a weed this year," you'll be able to prove it!*

Here's how to make a **HEIGHT CHART** for your class.

▪ Start with a length of butcher paper. Tape it to the wall in a position where the top of a student's head can be marked but there is still room to mark growth above. (See illustration.) Measure the distance from the floor to the bottom of the butcher paper and make a note of that measurement on the chart. Each time you tape the chart to the wall to remeasure, the distance should be exactly the same. Be sure kids names are written below their measurement area on the chart.

▪ After you have marked each child's height on the chart (you may need to use several lengths of paper), provide students with measurement tools and ask them to write their height in feet and inches (or meters and centimeters) on the line. Repeat that procedure after each measurement.

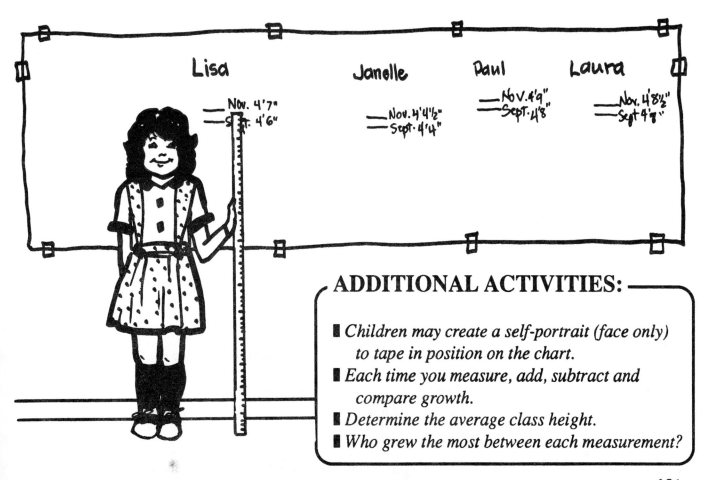

ADDITIONAL ACTIVITIES:

▪ *Children may create a self-portrait (face only) to tape in position on the chart.*
▪ *Each time you measure, add, subtract and compare growth.*
▪ *Determine the average class height.*
▪ *Who grew the most between each measurement?*

Mail Call

Encourage students to correspond with you and classmates throughout the year. The benefits are many. You will learn more about the young people who spend so much time in your classroom, friendships will be bonded and conflicts resolved. It's a great way to send personal, motivational messages. Plus children will have ample opportunity to practice writing skills.

Set up a classroom mail center in 5 easy steps.

Mountain School Lane

Kristi Lindsey Amy
Garrett Tyler Leanne Katie Quint
Caitlin Linda Ryan Marie Jennefer Tim

1. Teacher Mail:

Recycle a discarded mailbox, complete with flag, to set on your desk or other designated area. Use bright paint to print your name in an inviting and cheery welcome.

2. Student Mail:

For each mailbox, cut the top off a clean cardboard or plastic milk carton. Tape the sides of the cartons together. Continue to stack and tape the cartons in rows and columns to achieve the size and shape you need to fit the available space. Label each carton with a student name tag.

3. As a class, decide on a street name for your mailboxes. Create a sign to post nearby.

4. Explain the mail guidelines to the students:
- Notes must be positive. No unkind comments are allowed.
- All notes must be signed.
- Spelling and punctuation are not important. The message is!
- Write about anything—special feelings, a concern, an apology.
- Try to write back.

5. Reproduce a stack of attractive notepaper (following) to spark student interest.

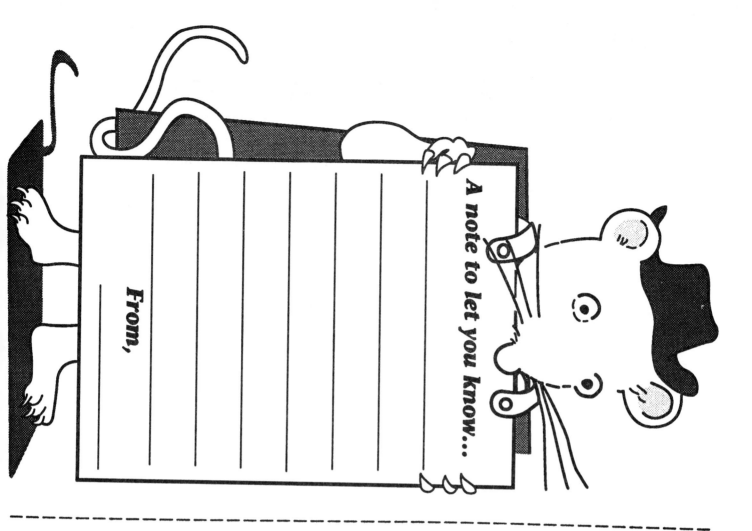

A note to let you know...

From,

A Special Message to:
(check the boxes that apply)

☐ My teacher   ☐ My old friend
☐ Study Buddy   ☐ My new friend
☐ Someone I'd like to know better

From,

Memory Book

> *Make a folding book following the directions below.*
> *Each month students illustrate their most memorable experience during the month.*
> *They can also write a sentence or short paragraph about it. They'll wind up with a*
> *super school-year souvenir.*

Materials

2-8"x 8" cardboard (21cm x 21cm)
wallpaper or giftwrap
white butcher paper 6"x 66" (15cm x 165cm)
scissors
glue
markers or crayons
ruler

Directions

• Cover the cardboard with giftwrap.

• Measure and mark every 6 inches (15cm)
  along the length of the butcher paper.

• Accordian fold on the marks.

• Glue each end of the butcher paper panel
  to the cardboard.

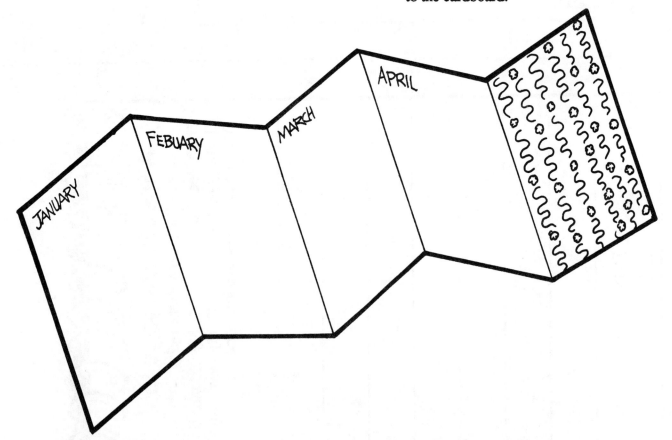

Each month, decorate a different section of the panel, working in order from front to back. You
may wish to use different medium each month to record the memories. For example, watercolors
in September, bright crayons in October, tissue paper in November, construction paper in December and so on.

LOBBY FOR A HOBBY

A hobby can be almost anything a person likes to do in his spare time. There are many kinds of hobbies—collections, sports and games, handicrafts. Hobbies offer enjoyment, knowledge and shared interests.

Encourage your students to start a "collection" hobby if they don't already have one. Having a collection will help your students fill their spare time constructively. Plan some hobby-sharing time throughout the year when students can bring their collections to class to share with their classmates.

Help your students find a hobby that interests them. Use the list below as a source. Ask them for their ideas, too.

Discuss ways they might display their collection. Remind them that the display does not have to be elaborate. Encourage them to gather books and information on the items in their collections.

HOBBY POSSIBILITIES

autographs	buttons	dried flowers
models	paper dolls	dolls
shells	stamps	coins
insects	butterflies	sports trading cards
bottles	bells	greeting cards
rocks and stones	matchbook covers	miniatures
postcards	photographs	salt & pepper shakers
baskets	newspaper clippings	colored glass
playing cards	costume jewelry	decals
stickers	bumper stickers	rubber stamps
types of lace	handkerchiefs	catalogs
mugs	ornaments	advertisements
pennants	hats	ticket stubs

BE A PAL

> *Make arrangements with another class—across town or across the country—to establish "sharing pals."*

Each month, set aside some time for each student to prepare something to send to their pal in the other class.

Use your imagination when establishing an exchange program. While **Pen Pals** are fun and can write letters back and forth, there are other exciting options too.

Art Pals

Exchange drawings, original artwork

Photo Pals

Send personal photos or photos of classroom events with a written description.

Exchange postcards showing your home town and its special attractions with out-of-town pals.

Holiday Pals

Exchange Halloween, Thanksgiving, Hanukkah, Christmas and Valentine cards. Make designs of your own creation. Or exchange a small handmade item appropriate for the holiday such as an ornament or placemat.

Secret Pals

Arrange for a pal in a nearby school! Don't identify yourself, but **do** describe yourself and your interests. Then plan a picnic in the spring and get together with the other class.

Try dressing in a way that might help your pal easily identify you. For example, if you wrote you love to dance, wear a leotard to the picnic. Find out your pal's food favorites and take along a specially-prepared lunch for him or her.

Book Pals

Exchange a book you have read. Compare your thoughts about the book the following month and send along another. This is a super way to recycle, too!

More than a Door

> *Transform the inside of your classroom door into a delightful welcome for all who enter the room.*
>
> *Divide into small groups. Each will be responsible for planning and decorating one month during the year.*

Here are the steps each group should follow
for successful door decorating:

Decide on a theme—holiday...patriotic...seasonal...subject

Make several sketches

Decide on wording, if any

Plan materials needed

Divide jobs and make a schedule

Assemble materials on the door

Read a Winner

Among the many books published for children only a small percentage have the distinction of being named Caldecott and Newbery Medal winners. (See listings in the INFORMATION INVENTORY.)

Young and old alike will delight in seeing the pictures and hearing these stories read aloud.

Make it a goal to share as many of these award-winning books with your students as possible.

Here are some suggestions to help you reach that goal.

INVOLVE PARENTS

Let parents know about your "award-winning" plan. Back-to-School night might be just the perfect time. Or, you may choose to send home a letter. Provide them with copies of the award-winners: Reproduce the pages from INFORMATION INVENTORY. They might wish to obtain their own copies as loans from the library or purchases for a home collection. The books are also super gifts to give for a classmate's (or your own) birthday. Find time to share the books together at home.

A BOOK A WEEK

CHOOSE one book a week, from the list of award-winners, to read to your class. You may even want to involve children in the selection process. Take a field trip to the library and ask the librarian to have ready as many of the books as possible. Then set a "reading priority" order.

FEATURE the book on a special table in your classroom. Try to have several copies on hand for children to look through and reread.

Reproduce a supply of the certificate (following) on colorful paper, complete the information, put it in a picture frame and set it on the table along with the book(s).

INTEGRATE the book into your curriculum. Plan art, writing and role playing based on the book.

Caldecott Medal Winner

_____

Book Title

_____

Author

_____

Year of Award

Newbery Medal Winner

_____

Book Title

_____

Author

_____

Year of Award

STORY HOUR

INCORPORATE cross-level teaching with a classroom program "Award-winning Story Hour".
Let other teachers know the day of the week and time that your students will be available to read these special books to younger students, either individually or in small groups. If the "younger students" are *yours,* ask parent volunteers to come in and do the same.

BOOK OF THE MONTH CLUB

ENCOURAGE students to read the books on their own. There are just too many on the lists to read them all in one school year. Let children know, in advance, which books you plan on reading aloud so that they might choose others. Then post the list of books (from INFORMATION INVENTORY) on an information bulletin board.

Students can become members of the BOOK OF THE MONTH CLUB by reading and reporting on one award-winning book sometime during the month.

BOOK OF THE MONTH CLUB members may want to:

- ↪ have meetings to discuss and make recommendations about the books they have read.
- ↪ design and make a membership card or use the sample, following, reproduced on index stock and cut into cards.
- ↪ plan special *"read-and-eat lunches"* to enjoy together.

BOOK OF THE MONTH CLUB

Award-Winning Book Readers

Member since

_____

_____
Name

Present this card for special member privileges.

BOOK OF THE MONTH CLUB

Award-Winning Book Readers

Member since

_____

_____
Name

Present this card for special member privileges.

BOOK OF THE MONTH CLUB

Award-Winning Book Readers

Member since

_____

_____
Name

Present this card for special member privileges.

BOOK OF THE MONTH CLUB

Award-Winning Book Readers

Member since

_____

_____
Name

Present this card for special member privileges.

BOOK OF THE MONTH CLUB

Award-Winning Book Readers

Member since

_____

_____
Name

Present this card for special member privileges.

BOOK OF THE MONTH CLUB

Award-Winning Book Readers

Member since

_____

_____
Name

Present this card for special member privileges.

BOOK OF THE MONTH CLUB

Award-Winning Book Readers

Member since

_____

_____
Name

Present this card for special member privileges.

BOOK OF THE MONTH CLUB

Award-Winning Book Readers

Member since

_____

_____
Name

Present this card for special member privileges.

BOOK OF THE MONTH CLUB

Award-Winning Book Readers

Member since

_____

_____
Name

Present this card for special member privileges.

BOOK OF THE MONTH CLUB

Award-Winning Book Readers

Member since

_____

_____
Name

Present this card for special member privileges.

Personal Dictionary

A good vocabulary leads to more confident and expressive writing and communication. And good vocabulary resources make this learning process more successful. Stock your classroom with adequate copies of dictionaries, rhyming dictionaries and Thesauruses (a great word for students to know).

You might also request that each student bring a home-supplied copy of any or all of these resources for quick referral.

Encourage children to add to their vocabulary by developing personal dictionaries. They can check here for spelling, synonyms, usage and more.

Here are some suggestions for personal dictionaries to keep handy on desktops. If vocabulary is "fingertip-handy" vocabularies will GROW!

File words in a box . . .

Ask parents to recycle a recipe box. Students can make their own dividers out of index cards with a colored-category tab taped on.

Divide words alphabetically. On each index card, decide which information you would like your students to include—spelling, definition, sentence showing usage, synonyms, antonyms, syllabication, rhyming words, etc.

Younger students may list a number of words on one card for spelling checks only. Older students may have a card for each word. Customize the format to suit student needs.

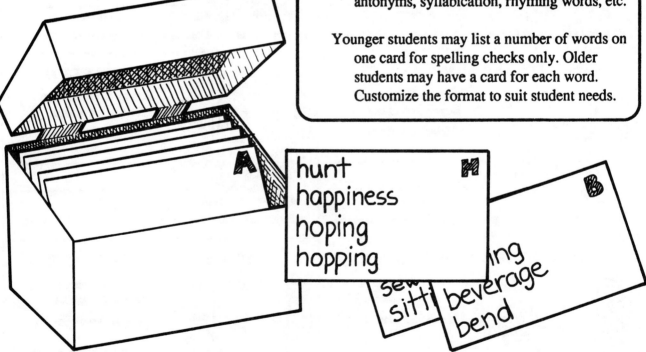

Jot words in a journal . . .

Reproduce following journal page—or design one with your class. Print pages back to back then fold and staple into a journal with a sufficient number of pages for each letter of the alphabet.

Students customize covers, add alphabet letter to each box.

Hang words on a ring . . .

Provide each child with a large metal ring. Hole-punch index cards, one for each letter of the alphabet, and hang the cards on the ring. More cards can be added as dictionaries grow. Just open the ring and add the card in the correct alphabetical position.

Hook your dictionary rings to a chair for classroom use or through a notebook ring for easy back-and-forth -to-school transportation!

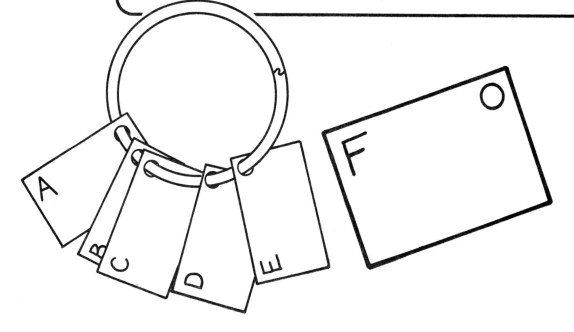

Cover Ups

Kids are always excited when a new textbook is handed out. Capitalize on the excitement and talk to your students about the care and protection of these valuable and expensive books.

Show students how to make a book cover. Then every time an old cover wears out or a new book is issued, they'll be ready to tackle the project on their own.

And while they're at it, they can learn about and apply the elements of good cover design for a book. So the project is not only useful, but fun and creative, too!

Follow the illustrated steps to making a book cover. Sturdy materials to use include brown shopping bags (a super recycler), white freezer paper, butcher paper, shelf paper and wallpaper.

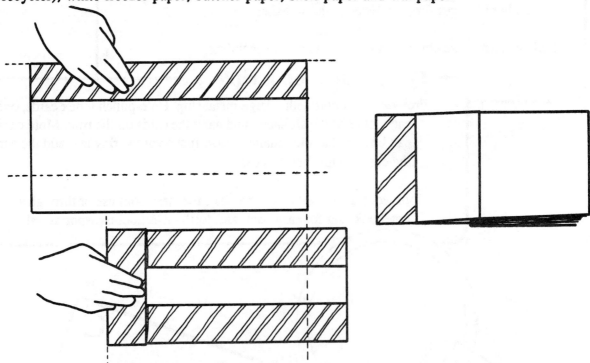

Now use crayons or markers to design the book cover. Remember these important design elements.

A book cover should:

1. Attract attention
2. Say what the book is about
3. Display the title and author's name
4. Show an interest graphic that reveals the content.

GROUP GRAPH

• Use yarn to create a large grid on a classroom wall or bulletin board. Start the grid low to the ground and make it no higher than the children can reach.

• Fill a box with colored construction paper cut to fit inside the grid squares. Place the box near the grid along with tape or push pins for attaching the squares to the grid.

• Discuss the use of a bar graph and how data is logged.

Children can record their choices during opening, free time or at specified times during the day, by taping construction paper in a square on the grid.

Take time to talk about the choices. This is a great way to find out about children, their likes, dislikes and concerns.

Other hints:
Change subjects to suit holiday or time of year. Ask children to participate in choosing subject and labeling columns.

Frequently change the subject and column headings. Children can be involved in the choices.
Some suggestions:
Favorite sports: baseball, hockey, soccer, football, swimming, other
How are you feeling today?   grumpy, happy, tired, excited, worried, other

Birthday month

Favorite toy: doll, rocket, jumprope, bicycle, skates, skateboard
Favorite dessert: cookies, cake, pie, ice cream, pudding, other
Weather preferences: cloudy, raining, snowing, sunny, windy
Always include a column for **OTHER**.

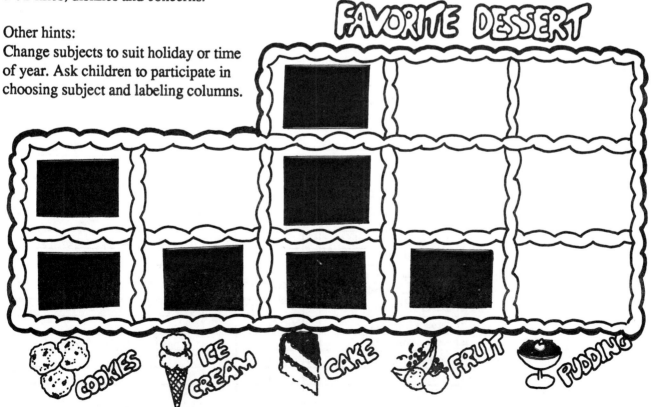

Motor Skill Checklist

Use the form on the following page to prepare a checklist of motor development skills appropriate to your students and grade level. Assemble each student record in a notebook to make referencing and record keeping easier. Pretest at the start of the school year, track individual progress during the year and posttest near the end of the school year.

The checklist will:

- **Provide** direction for your outdoor physical education program
- **Serve** as a conference and parent involvement tool
- **Assist** your planning for individual needs
- **Signal** developmental needs

Use the checklist key to indicate:

- test dates
- a mastered skill
- the date the student exhibited mastery
- an area of special need

Use the checklist note area to:

- **Tell** parents how they can help
- **Make** special reminders to yourself regarding a "help" plan
- **Indicate** exceptional ability
- **Record** observations

Include skills that you want students to master during the year. Check with your school district curriculum guidelines for help in setting your goals.

Continue to provide extra practice for students with individual needs with parent and classroom aide assistance. Checklists can be photocopied and sent home periodically so that parents are kept aware of student needs and progress. The checklist can also be included in the student's personal records.

Here's a sample chart prepared for a first grade class:

Motor Skill Checklist

Key: ☒ Mastered ☒ Area of special need   Student Steven Smith   Grade 1

	Skill	Test dates 9/27	11/25	1/20				Date of Mastery	Notes
1.	tie a bow								9/27 not introduced
2.	skip	X						9/27	
3.	hop on one foot		X						
4.	hold scissors correctly	N							needs help w/sm. motor d.
5.	cut on a line			N					
6.	hold a pencil correctly	N							
7.	catch a rolling ball			X					
8.	run in a relay race	X						9/27	
9.	throw a large ball		X						
10.	catch a large ball								wk. on eye/hand co-ord.
11.	bounce a large ball	X						9/27	
12.									

Motor Skill Checklist

Key: ☒ Mastered ☒ Area of special need

Student _____ Grade _____

Skill	Test dates								Date of Mastery	Notes
1.										
2.										
3.										
4.										
5.										
6.										
7.										
8.										
9.										
10.										
11.										
12.										
13.										
14.										
15.										
16.										
17.										
18.										

Safe-keeping for Art

Follow the instructions below to make a large portfolio. Store special art projects in it that are completed throughout the year.

Share your portfolio contents during Open House. OR plan a special "Welcome to our Studio" day where portfolios are shared with other students and invited guests. Serve "Pointilism Punch" and "Impressionist Cookies".

Directions:

Start with a large sheet of butcher paper—24" (60 cm) x 36" (90 cm).

Fold one edge to within 6" (15 cm) of the opposite end.

Staple, glue or punch holes and thread with yarn to close the sides.

Fold over the top flap. Secure with a small piece of Velcro held with contact cement.

A Stitch in Time

Learn about timelines and chronological events with this cooperative project. This display stays up all year and makes a super object of conversation at Open House night, too!

Use yarn to create timeline boxes across a wall (see illustration).

Label each box, starting with the first month of school and ending with the last.

A group of students is responsible for filling in each month's box with memorable classroom events during the month. This can be done in writing and with pictures. Groups can be organized at the beginning of the year or names drawn at the start of each month. Students can be involved in choosing the selection process to be used.

Get Going with Games

Here are some games to get children acquainted, meet and make new friends and learn more about each other.

— SUMMER RUN —

Head outside for this one! Ask students to make one long, horizontal line. Establish another line about 15 feet away.

Call out summer activities. For example:
- visited your grandparents
- rode a horse
- rode your bike
- relaxed in a hammock
- went swimming

When a child hears something he or she did during the summer he/she races to the line and back to the start.

Call only one activity at a time. Wait for all kids to return to the start before calling another.

Stop occasionally to ask a child to share some more information about that event. (This will help keep the kids from running for things they did **not** do!)

— AT THE TONE... —

During the first week, tell children to be listening for a certain signal—a bell, a buzzer, a handclap, for instance. When they hear the signal they pack up all their belongings and choose a new seat.

The only rule is that the new seat must be next to someone they haven't sat next to before.

Once at the seat, children introduce themselves to the person seated on each side and share one fact about themselves.

This will help you establish final seating arrangements for the class and keep children listening and looking forward to the signal! Maybe they'll make a new friend, too!

Vacation Charade

Ask students to wrte an activity they did during vacation on an index card.

Put all the cards in a box.

Ask willing students to reach inside the box, draw a card, and act out the activity.

After the activity has been identified, ask the writer to share a few more details about the event.

Add a Letter

Learn to spell classmates' names.

One student is asked to stand (no name, please.)

Another student goes to the chalkboard, writes the first letter of that student's name then taps another student and sits down.

The student tapped goes to the chalkboard and writes the next letter in the student's name. The process is repeated. If a student is incorrect he or she simply chooses another person to go to the board.

Score classroom points for each name spelled correctly.

Variations: Pick a category such as
   Items found in a classroom
   Things on a playground
   School subjects
   Food in a lunchbox

See if students can develop words to fit into the category.

Boxed Games

> *Recycle all those gift, jewelry and shoe boxes into useful classroom teaching tools. A few hours of preparation on your part will provide kids with hours of stimulating learning fun.*

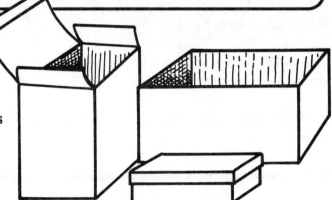

Boxed games will come in handy as:

- free-time fillers
- instant activities for substitute teachers
- constructive morning openers
- easy-to-assemble learning centers

Older students can help assemble games, decorate boxes and create games of their own to add to the classroom collection. This would be a super, on-going extra credit opportunity.

The following pages are filled with simple games that will fit neatly inside a box. Choose from the suggestions or create some of your own. Here's what to do.

Boxed-Game Basics

Bring boxes from home. Any size will work. The more variety, the better. Remember, good things come in small packages (and big ones, too!).

Decorate each box. Colorful boxes will spark student interest.

Name each game. Use your imagination to create names that sound like fun!

Laminate paper game parts. Increase the life of each game. Keep an inventory of game parts inside each box lid to avoid losing parts.

Play the game with your students. Be sure they know the rules before the game is introduced to the classroom collection. As students create games on their own they can get some practice in oral presentation by instructing classmates in the rules.

Boxed Games

Contraction Matchup

Objective: Matching contractions and their base words

To Make:
Cut ten medium-sized circles from construction paper.
Use a marking pen to make a zig-zag line through each circle.
On one half write a contraction. On the other half, write the
   words that make the contraction.
Cut along the zig-zag line.

To Play: Match the contraction halves.

Variations: compound words, math facts, foreign language

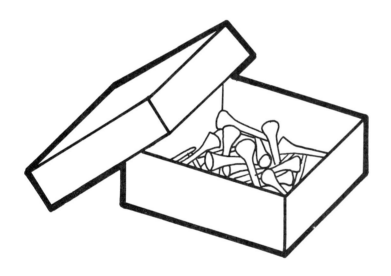

Fits to a Tee

Objective: Classifying

To Make:
Fill a small box with assorted colored golf
   tees.

To Play: Sort by color into piles.

Get-Togethers

Objective: Object association

To Make:
Cut out magazine pictures of individual items that are
   associated such as *bread* and *butter*, *shoe* and *sock*,
   flowers and *vase*.
Glue each picture to an index card.

To Play: Match the card pairs that go together.

Boxed Games

Get Rolling

Objective: Finding the sum of several numbers

To Make:
3 or more die depending on the student age

To Play: Two or more players. Roll the dice. Add the numbers that show on the dice. The first to whisper the correct sum scores a point.

Variations: Rearrange the dice from left to right in numerical order.

Spin a Yarn

Objective: reproducing yarn shape; developing eye-hand coordination

To Make:
Cut assorted colors of yarn about one yard (one meter) in length. Some should be tied at the ends, others not.

To Play: Two players. One creates an open or closed shape with a length of yarn. The second attempts to recreate the shape **exactly** with a second length of yarn.

Variations:
Use two different colors yarn.
Make a shape with a designated number of curves.
Use one length of yarn tied at the end and one not.
Set a time limit for recreating the shape.

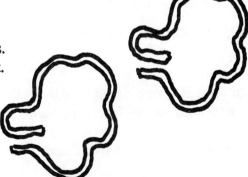

Boxed Games

Category Cards

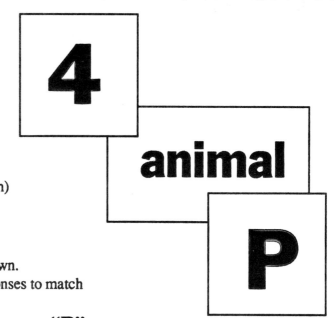

Objective: Categorizing, thinking skills

To Make:
Create three sets of category cards—
    — letters
    — numbers (1 through 6, several of each)
    — categories

To Play:
Sort the cards into three piles. Set them face down.
Turn over the top card on each pile. Write responses to match
the information on the cards.

For example: Name 4 animals beginning with the letter **"P"**.

Scoring: Award a point for each correct response. Award an additional point to the player who has
the most correct responses. Award another point to each player who has as many responses as shown on
the number card.

Ins and Outs

Objective: Writing number equations

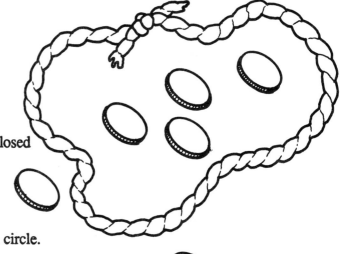

To Make:
Cut a length of yarn (about 36 inches). Tie to form a closed
piece.
12 colored chips

To Play:
Hold a handful of chips about 8 inches above the yarn circle.
Drop the chips.
Write a math equation to show the sum of the chips inside
plus the chips outside the circle.
    (Chips landing on the yarn are considered in.)

Repeat the "drop" with the same number of
chips. How many different equations were created?

Example:

INS	+	OUTS		
4	+	3	=	7

Ground Grids

> *Create two large grids on the ground—one outdoors on the playground and one indoors on the classroom floor—and you'll have the basics for a variety of games to play all year long. Play the games suggested here, then let students make up some of their own.*

OUTDOOR GRID

CONSTRUCTION

Paint a 16-square grid in an 8'x8' area. (Squares need to be large enough for children to have room for physical activity.)

Paint a large, colorful number in each square. Vary the colors and keep them between 0 through 10.

GAME IDEAS

FOLLOW IT

Call out directions. Ask students to follow.
"Hop clockwise around the outside squares."
"Jump through the numbers in this order; two, five, ten, two.

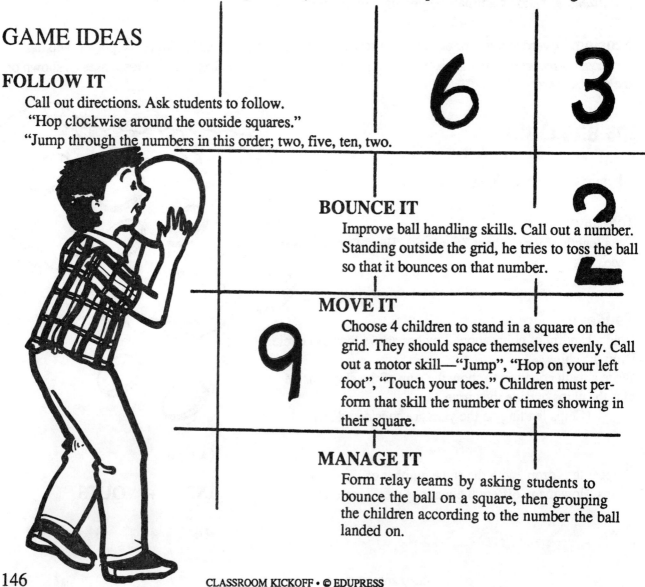

BOUNCE IT

Improve ball handling skills. Call out a number. Standing outside the grid, he tries to toss the ball so that it bounces on that number.

MOVE IT

Choose 4 children to stand in a square on the grid. They should space themselves evenly. Call out a motor skill—"Jump", "Hop on your left foot", "Touch your toes." Children must perform that skill the number of times showing in their square.

MANAGE IT

Form relay teams by asking students to bounce the ball on a square, then grouping the children according to the number the ball landed on.

Ground Grids

INDOOR GRID

CONSTRUCTION

Clear an area approximately 4x4. Use masking or electrical tape to create a grid of 16 equal-size squares.

Keep additional numbers and letters, printed on index cards, on hand to use for some of the games.

GAME IDEAS

TOSS IT

Math Toss—Tape index card *numbers* (appropriate to student learning level) inside each square. Toss a *beanbag* to solve a flash card problem, indicate number recognition, match numbers to number words.

Word Toss—Tape index card *letters* inside each square. Toss a *beanbag* to spell words.

GRAPH IT

Reinforce graphing skills with a hands-on graphing game. Label each grid column (either horizontal or vertical) with a category. Call out an item. Student puts construction paper "marker" in the corresponding graph column.

COORDINATE IT

Call out number coordinates. Ask a student to stand on that coordinate point on the grid. Call out another coordinate. Another student stands on *that* point. Repeat this several times. Students stretch yarn between them to show the resulting graph.

MANAGE IT

Use the grid to help with classroom management. For example:

"When you're finished with your work, sit in a square on the grid." First five people standing on the grid go to recess before the others.

"All those wearing purple, stand in a square on the grid." Here's a cooperative learning group.

CATEGORIZE IT

Provide students with a junk box, filled with a variety of items—from stuffed animals to bows. Students sort items into categories by putting like-items in the same square on the grid.

Recess . . . INDOORS!

Do the rainy-day blues have your class feeling low? Here are some out-of-the-ordinary games to lift foul-weather spirits.

Shoe Toss

Everyone takes off their right shoe and lines the heel up against the wall.

Divide into several teams.

Players get a chance to toss a ping-pong ball at the shoes. If the ball lands and stays in a shoe that team scores a point.

Hide in Plain Sight

Choose a student to hide an eraser in the classroom. The only rule is that **part** of the eraser **must be visible** to class members.

As a variation choose two or three students to hide erasers at the same time.

Players open their eyes and look around the room for the eraser. When they have seen it, they fold their arms in front of them.

Wait a minute or so, ask someone to reveal the eraser's location and begin the game again.

Recess . . .
INDOORS!

Hat Pass

Keep a box of hats handy for this game.

Players sit in a circle, shoulders touching. Each wears a funny hat.

When the **caller** says "Hats, left" or "Hats, right" each player takes off his hat and places it on the head of the person on that side of him.

When the **caller** says "Hats off" player take off their hat and hold it in their hands.

When the **caller** says "Hats on" hats remain on the player's head.

Anyone who misses takes off his hat and sets it on the floor in front of him.

Continue until one player remains.

Silent Speed Ball

Play this game indoors with a ball of yarn. Children stand at their desk, behind their chair. The yarn ball is tossed from one player to another. Once caught, that player quickly tosses the yarn ball to another player.

If a student touches the yarn ball and does not catch it, he sits down. The last one standing is declared the winner.

It's a good idea to have a "referee" for this game. If a yarn ball is not thrown accurately or if there is any dispute as to whether or not a player touched the ball, the referee can resolve the problem.

KEEPING SCORE

Anyone can keep score using paper and pencil. But what can you do if those two items are not at hand when it's time to keep track of a game score? Here are some imaginative ways to do just that!

Tie 'em In Knots

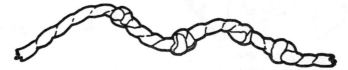

Each team gets a length of yarn.
The scorekeeper ties a knot in the team's yarn for each point scored.

Roll 'em Up

Roll bits of newspaper or tissue into tiny balls.
When a team scores a point, put a ball on their side of a scorecard.

Rock 'em

Before play begins, gather small stones and rocks.
A team is awarded a rock for each point scored.

Spoon 'em

Each time a team scores a point, a level tablespoon of soft dirt is put in a pile. The team with the biggest pile wins!

Teaching TIP

Give your class a chance to come up with some imaginative ways to keep score on their own. Then implement those ways into your game playing.

Games . . . Old and New

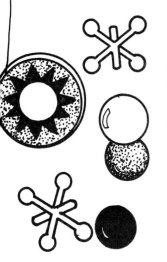

Some games that you enjoy and play today were popular when your parents were your age. But sometimes a favorite game enjoyed by a parent can be one you never heard of and vice-versa!

Compare your favorite games with those your parents enjoyed as children. Spend a few minutes "interviewing" them— or two other adults—and record their answers in the space provided. Ask them to show you how to play some of the games you are unfamiliar with.

When you return to school with your completed list, compare your parents' responses with the responses your classmates' received. Spend some time teaching each other these games and playing them, too! You **might be surprised** at how much fun they are!

Type of Game	Favorites		
	Mine	Mom's	Dad's
1. Indoor Game			
2. Ball Game (team)			
3. Ball Game (1 or 2 players)			
4. Game of skill using equipment— (yo-yo, marbles, jacks)			
5. Board Game			
6. Best Game Skill— throwing, kicking, etc.			
7. Best Game to Watch.			

Get Going with Games

Stopwatch Games

An inexpensive purchase can can be worth its' weight in gold! Keep a stopwatch in your desk for games to play "at a moment's notice."

INDOOR

Learning Games

How fast can you...

Say the alphabet?
Write five, 3-letter words—all spelled correctly?
Complete 50 simple addition (or subtraction, multiplication, division) problems?
Tie both shoelaces in a bow?
Find a word in the dictionary. . . a subject in the encyclopedia?

How long does it take...

To write your name neatly compared to messy?
To walk, heel to toe, from one side of the classroom to the other?
For an ice cube to melt?
For water to boil?

Management Games

How fast can you...

Get ready to go home?
Clean up for recess?
Clean up a project?
(Keep the number in a circle on the chalkboard.
Students will have fun trying to beat their class record.)
Pass out (or collect) papers?
Gather library books?
Respond to a fire drill?

How long can you...

Work without talking to your "neighbor"?
Work without asking for help (when you can find the answer yourself)?
Go with no "tattling"?

Stopwatch Games

OUTDOOR

Skill Games

How fast can you...

Run the bases?
Complete an obstacle course?
Do ten chin-ups?
Run the length of a soccer field?
Run a relay race?
Complete 25 jumping jacks?

How long does it take...

To build a snowman?
To make three snowballs?
To play a quarter of soccer?
For the class to find ten hidden objects?
To turn a jump rope fifty times?
Dribble a basketball the length of the court?

Management Games

How fast can you...

Line up after recess is over?
Put away the playground equipment?
Clean up after eating lunch?
Get ready for an outdoor activity?

How long can you...

Stay in line without pushing or arguing with classmates?
Walk to the playground without running?
Do sit-ups (or jumping jacks, or toe touches) without stopping?
Wait for the bus without talking?

Get Going with Games

Create a set of numeral flash cards, 0-50. Make the numbers large enough that the entire class will be able to see them from a distance. Then choose from the games below and gear them to your students' learning level. You'll always be ready for math games...

In a FLASH!

Number Recognition:

• Use as flash cards for direct response to number shown.

• Show child two or more cards. Say one of the numbers shown. Ask child to select the correct number card.

• Sort cards by a given number. Example: "Find every card that has a '3' on it."

• Advanced number recognition can be practiced by selecting two or more 2-digit number cards and placing them end to end. Child rewrites number, inserting comma in the correct position and then reads number orally.

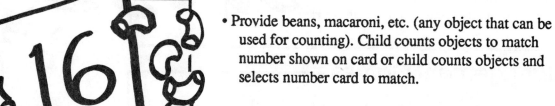

Counting:

• Provide beans, macaroni, etc. (any object that can be used for counting). Child counts objects to match number shown on card or child counts objects and selects number card to match.

• Scramble number cards. Child unscrambles and places number cards in correct sequential counting order, either forward or backward.

• Place cards in counting order by 2's, 3's, 5's and 10's.

Memory Development:

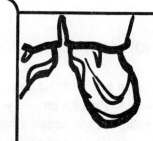

• Place 2 or more cards in any order. Scramble the cards and ask child to replace them in the *same* order.

• Show a group of cards. Number of cards and length of time shown can be increased in difficulty according to age and ability. Remove the cards. Ask the child to verbally repeat or write the numbers that were shown.

Number Concepts:—— In a FLASH!

Highest, Lowest (Greater than, Less than):

- From 2 or more cards, child selects which one is higher (highest), lower (lowest).

- From 2 cards, child selects which one is greater than the other, less than the other.

- Unscramble a group of cards and place them in order from lowest to highest (or highest to lowest).

- Sort cards into "even" and "odd" number piles. Hold card up for "even" or "odd" response.

Place value:

- "Which number is the ones place? the tens?" Select 2 or more 2-digit cards. Show as one numeral by putting cards end to end. Child points to and names place values (ones, tens, etc.) *or* ask, "Which number is in the hundreds place," etc.

Addition, Subtraction, Multiplication, Division drill:

These can be individual, group, ore team activities. Gear number card selection to the child's (children's) ability level.

- Hold up 2 cards. Child adds, subtracts, multiplies or divides and responds verbally or in writing. (Point can be scored for each correct response.)

- Child selects 3 or more cards, then rewrites numbers and completes column addition problem.

Listen Closely

Here are some easy listening games to play in an instant.

Tick Tock

Hide a loud, ticking alarm clock somewhere in the classroom. Children tiptoe around and try to determine the location of the clock.

When they think they know the location they return to their seats.

Everyone shares their answer.

Tap It Twice

Everyone puts their head on their desk. One person uses a pencil to tap twice on some object in the room.

If a player thinks he can name the object being tapped he raises his hand. If the answer is incorrect he is out of the game and the object is tapped again. If correct he becomes the "tapper."

Can You Tell What Fell?

Children sit with their backs to a table. Drop an object such as a coin, paper clip, spoon, button or comb on the table.

Who can guess what was dropped?

Toss and Listen

Stand in a large circle. Toss a beanbag to someone who must then recite one safety or class rule. That player then tosses the beanbag to someone else who recites a different rule. The game continues. A rule CANNOT be repeated. If a player repeats he or she sits down and is out of the game.

Mystery Game

Here's a simple game that will adapt to any situation, holiday or unit of study! Play it once. Then play it often!

How To Play:

Choose a theme for the game (see below).

Each player has an identity, clue, location etc., related to the theme, taped to his or her back. (Mystery clues can be teacher or student created.) Younger players may have picture instead of word clues.

The player's task is to find out, by asking questions posed to classmates, what is written on the card taped to their back. The questions should be answered with one or two-word responses. Older students may only ask questions that can be answered with "yes" or "no" responses.

For Example:

Theme: WELCOME BACK TO SCHOOL
Mystery clue: chalkboard
Possible student questions:
    Am I found in the classroom?
    Can you write on me?
    What color am I?

Mystery Game Subjects:

Here are some game themes with a few mystery clues give you the idea…

Welcome Back To School—chalkboard, desk, teacher, school bus, swing, principal, cafeteria
Halloween—mask, costume, witch, pumpkin, jack-o' lantern, candy, haunted house, skeleton
Animals—bear, gorilla, lion, tiger, monkey, leopard, elephant, giraffe, rhinoceros
Famous Holiday People—George Washington, Cupid, Christopher Columbus, Santa Claus
BIG Things—elephant, giant, blimp, hippopotamus, moon, Empire State Building

Project Planner

On Tour

*These activities will help new students learn more about their school.
And returning students may discover some things they never knew.*

Silent Observations

Take a silent tour of the school. Then divide into teams. Ask questions about things students may have seen on the walk. Score a point for each correct response.

For example, ask the students:

- Describe the vase on the librarian's desk.
- What was on the bulletin board in the main office.
- What was the principal wearing?
- How many potted plants were in the main office?

The silent tour can be repeated throughout the year.
Ask children to recall changes.

Progressive Lunch

Take a break from the standard lunch period and plan a progressive lunch. For example:

- Eat your sandwiches by the flagpole.
- Munch on fruit outside the library.
- Have dessert near the equipment room.

What are the chances of sharing lunch in the teacher's lounge or principal's office?

Share your observations, talk about changes, learn what goes on at each location.

On Tour

Coin and Class Hike

All you need for this school tour is a **coin** and a **class**! Start at your classroom door. To determine which direction to go, toss a coin in the air. If the coin lands on "heads", go *right*. If the coin lands on "tails", go *left*. Each time you come to a corner, a turn or a dead end, flip the coin.

As you travel on your coin tour, point out the various things you see—the office, library, bus loading zone. You may wind up passing the cafeteria several times but that's part of the fun! It's certain that by the time your class *and* their coin have completed their school tour, they will know their way around the school backwards and forwards—and left and right!

Interview Tour

Head out on a tour of the school "armed" with paper and pencil or tape recorder. Stop to "interview" every person you pass. It might be a student, the principal or a visiting parent.

During the interview, let the class ask **three** appropriate questions. Upon your return to class, review your notes or listen to the tape. Discuss the people you met and what you learned about them.

Project Planner

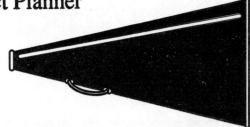

Be True To Your School

Three Cheers

Make up a rousing cheer about how great your school is.

Demonstrate and teach it to your classroom.

Display Your Mascot

Does your school have a mascot? The tigers? dolphins? vikings?

Set aside an area in your classroom to collect models and pictures of the mascot. Add to it all year.

If your school doesn't have a mascot, how about starting a schoolwide campaign to select one?

A Banner Year

Design a banner for your school. Hang it from the classroom ceiling.

Tour Guides

Create a map that shows all the points of interest in your school.

Reproduce copies of the map for visitors to use while on campus.

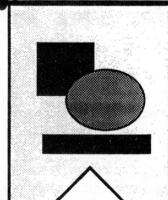

F.Y.I.

Write a short history of your school. How did it get its name? When was it built? Any special accomplishments?

Share this information in the office with visitors, guests, and newly enrolling students and their parents.

State Your State or Province

Combine geography with getting to know each other. On one classroom wall, make a large outline of the United States (or Canada). Students create dimensional details ...

sandpaper deserts
eggcarton cup mountains
fringed tissue forests

Give each student a pushpin tag with his or her name on it.

Throughout the year, students move the tags around to share information about:

- place of birth
- vacation destination
- places you would like to visit
- research or report assignments

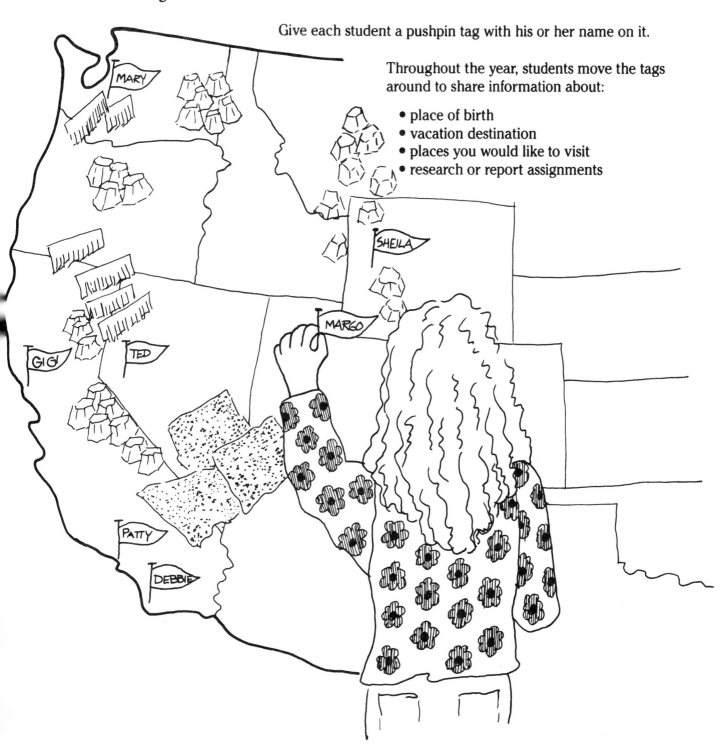

CALENDAR CARNIVAL

Here are two clever calendars to choose from. One is for a desktop, the other hangs on the wall. Kids can make them for their own use or give them as gifts.

DESKTOP CALENDAR

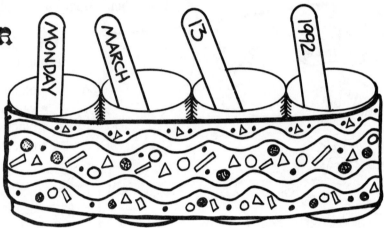

Materials
4 small cans of equal size
masking tape
contact paper
craft (popsicle) sticks
marking pen

Directions
1. Tape the cans together in one row.
2. Cover with contact paper cut to size.
3. Mark sticks, as shown, with the days of the week, months, dates and year.
   Be sure to use both sides and ends of the sticks.

Put the sticks in the cans, from left to right, to show the correct date.

WALL CALENDAR

- Decorate and glue four library pockets (available in stationery stores) to a strip of butcher paper.

- Mark index cards the same as the sticks were marked for the desktop calendar, above.

- Hang the calendar with yarn and insert the correct information in the pockets, reading from top to bottom.

A Picture's Worth a Thousand Projects

Well, maybe not a thousand, but some simple preparation will provide several activities filled with learning fun.

Preparation:

- Fold a large sheet of construction paper in half.

- On the left half, paste a magazine, travel brochure or catalog picture. It should have some detail.

- On the right half, write three questions about the picture.

- Write an identifying number on the back of each page.

1. What color is the fence?

2. How many windows in the picture?

3. How many stars are in the sky?

Total Recall

Play in pairs. Here are three variations:

☆ One partner studies the picture then gives it to his partner who reads the questions.

☆ One partner studies the picture then gives it to his partner who makes up and asks his own questions about the picture.

☆ Both partners study the picture then turn the picture over and take turns relating details about the picture. How many can they name?

Quick Captions

Children number a piece of paper from one to as many pictures as there are.

Each student is given a picture.

Allow one minute for them to write a caption for the picture next to its identifying number on their page.

At a signal, the picture is passed to another student and the process is repeated.

Spend some time sharing and comparing captions.

Project Planner

Mystery Me

Follow the clues to reveal the identity of the "Mystery Me." When projects are complete, collect them and pass them out to students at random. How many identities did they guess correctly?

Here are student instructions for two simple variations.

Windows

Draw or cut and paste magazine pictures of things that will give clues to your identity. These can be physical features (for example, color yellow hair if you are a blonde) or things you like to eat or do.

Position the pictures on construction paper according to the diagram. In the largest spot at the top, draw or paste a picture of yourself and write your name under the picture.

Cut windows, following the same diagram, in a second piece of colored construction paper and glue the edges to the paper with the picture clues. The windows, when opened, should reveal the picture underneath.

Lift Ups

Fold a piece of plain drawing paper in half, lengthwise.

At equal intervals, make four cuts from the open edge of one half to the fold (see illustration).

Under the flap on the far right, color or paste a picture of yourself. Under all the remaining flaps, paste or color pictures of clues to your identity.

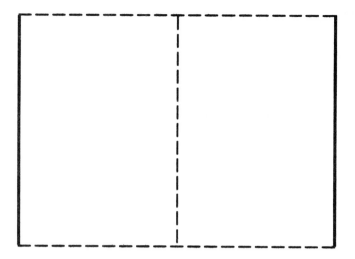

Mystery Me

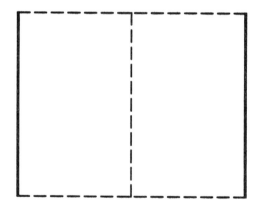

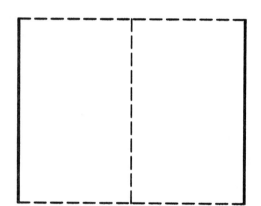

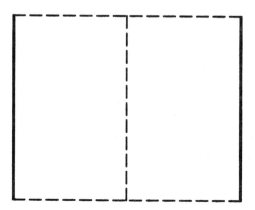

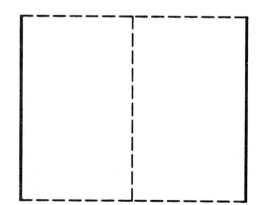

Partner Projects

Measurement becomes visual in this fun partner project.

How Long Is It?

Cut apart the "How Long?" cards on the following page. There are enough for a class of 32 children—16 pairs.

Divide children into pairs. Each pair selects at random a "How Long?" card. They keep the information on their card a secret. Discuss with students that the measurements are *average* lengths.

Provide measurement tools—ruler, yard stick, meter stick, measuring tapes—**and balls of string.**

Ask students to:

    1. Measure a length of string equal to the length on their "How Long?" card.
    2. Write three clues that would help identify what is on their card.
        Each clue should give easier information. For example:

        Giraffe's Neck
        1. This is found on an animal's body.
        2. The animal can look down on lots of other animals.
        3. This is found just below this animal's head.

When all this is completed, head outside for some fun. Each pair has a turn to stand up and stretch their length of yarn between them. They read their clues, one at a time, to the rest of the class who have a chance to guess the secret identity after each clue. Reveal the identity after the third clue.

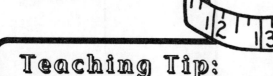

Teaching Tip:

Now that they know how to play, ask children to research new lengths to identify. This is an activity that is repeated many times throughout the school year.

How Long?
gray owl (smallest owl)
6 inches (15 cm)

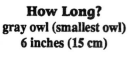

How Long?
violin—24 inches (60 cm)

How Long?
alligator—11 feet (3.3 meters)

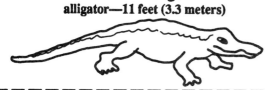

How Long?
beaver
4 feet (120 cm)

How Long?
Chihuahua (smallest dog)
5 inches (12.5 cm)

How Long?
roadrunner
2 feet (60 cm)

How Long?
Brontosaurus (longest dinosaur)
80 feet (24 meters)

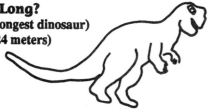

How Long?
Stegosaurus
20 feet (6 meters)

How Long?
swordfish—12 feet (4 meters)

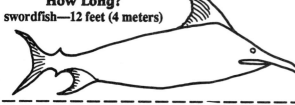

How Long?
oboe (musical instrument)—21 inches (53 cm)

How Long?
hippopotamus
15 feet (5.25 meters)

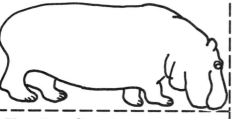

How Long?
lion
9 feet (3 meters)

How Long?
blue whale (largest animal ever!)—100 feet (30 meters)

How Long?
hockey stick—55 inches (140 cm)

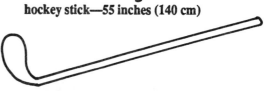

How Long?
diamondback rattlesnake—7 feet (2 meters)

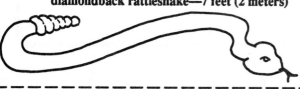

How Long?
adult elephant's trunk—5 feet (1.5 meters)

Partner Projects

Make a new friend and learn the ins and outs of working together. Here are some projects two people can do.

Sculpture Recycling

- Collect junk from home…containers, string, plastic throwaways.

- Work with your partner to staple, glue, tie or connect the junk into a freestanding sculpture.

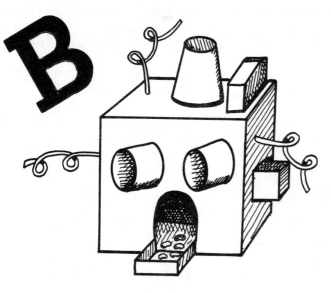

Alphabet Machines

- Each pair is given a letter of the alphabet cut from construction paper.

- Partners create an imaginary machine that does something beginning with their letter.

They must:
- Glue the letter to paper and illustrate their machine in action.

- Explain, either orally or written, how the machine works.

For example, an F machine that fries french fries or freezes fabric or creates fun.

Or an S machine that sorts socks, sneaks up on snow or stamps out soil.

Teaching Tip:

Turn this into a lesson verbs and nouns!

3-Part Plates

Picnic plates, with three divisions, lend themselves to several learning projects.

Plate Pets

Use your imagination to turn these plates into wonderful animals.

Suggestion:
cat, skunk, dog, lion

Sequencing Steps

Choose an event and illustrate the stages of growth in each section of the plate.

Suggestion:
seed, sprout, flower
baby, child, adult
key, ignition, drive

Compound Components

Illustrate compound words.
In the two top sections, draw the words within a compound word.

In the bottom section, illustrate the whole word.

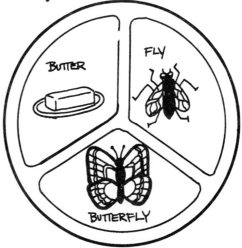

Project Planner

Wrap-Arounds

> *Get students interacting with each other with this project .*

Materials:

- ❧ cardboard tube from paper toweling or gift wrap
- ❧ length of colored yarn , thin ribbon or string
- ❧ assorted craft scraps such as poster board,
    beads, feathers, pipe cleaners, buttons, shell

Directions: (Each student needs to make 6 **identical** Wrap-Arounds.)

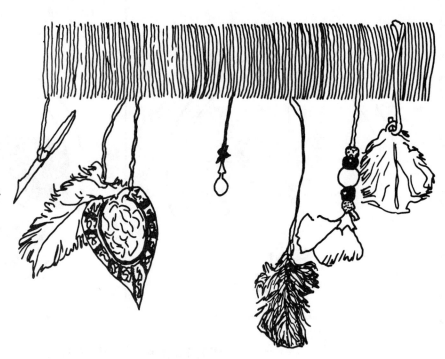

A Wrap-Around is made by tying an object to one end of a strand of yarn, ribbon or string. The object can be anything from a decorated paper heart or other shape, a few colored beads, a scrap of fringe or a pipe cleaner sculpture. Provide a variety of materials—kids will create wonderful things!

Children swap one of their own Wrap-Arounds for a classmate's and then wraps their tube with the newly traded Wrap-Around, finishing with the end that has the object attached. Be sure that the string is held in place by the wrapping.

As each strand of yarn nears its end, glue it to the tube a short distance from the yarn end.

— TEACHER TIPS —

- ❧ Children should end up with a fairly equal number of Wrap-Arounds on their tube.
- ❧ Trade for only one Wrap-Around a day—Look forward to the colorful additions!

CLASSROOM KICKOFF • © EDUPRESS

(Teacher Note: Reproduce a copy for each student to keep as reference. Make a sample poster together.)

POSTER DESIGN TIPS

*Sometimes you are asked to design and create a poster for a project, contest or campaign. If you are familiar with the elements of good poster design, the job will be much easier and more successful. Keep a copy of these **poster design tips** in your notebook or desk.*

⇨ ATTENTION GETTERS

◆ The most important information should **STAND OUT.**
◆ The headline or slogan should **attract attention**.
◆ The background should be uncluttered.

 ## ART

◆ Make it colorful.
◆ Use unusual photos and illustrations.

∅ WORDS AND LETTERS

◆ Use **BOLD** easy-to-read lettering.
◆ Don't write too much.
◆ The message should be clear.

Conservation Projects

Involve students in conservation projects throughout the school year to help them understand the problems of pollution and overuse in our environment. Make them an important part of the worldwide effort to help stop the damage and rebuild natural resources. Show them that even a small effort goes a long way toward caring for our environment.

These projects have been adapted from the following resources:

50 Simple Things KIDS can do to Save the Earth,
The EarthWorks Group, John Javna, Universal Press
2 Minutes a Day for a Greener Planet,
Marjorie Lamb, Harper & Row

Field Trips and Speakers

Visit a recycling center or water treatment plant.
Walk to the nearest park. Clean up the litter.
Invite a speaker from the water district or utility company to discuss conservation methods.

School-wide Projects

Start a **PROTECT YOUR ENVIRONMENT** (PYE) club in your school. Hold biweekly meetings to make new plans and evaluate old ones. Make club membership open to all ages for some super cross-teaching activities.

Plan a school-wide clean-up campaign. Be sure all trash is thrown in trash cans.

Send pictures, stories or new conservation ideas to *The Kids' EarthWorks Group*, 1400 Shattuck Avenue, #25, Berkeley, CA 94709

Help protect our endangered species. Ask your school's parent organization to provide funds for the school to **Adopt** an animal. For information write to the *American Association of Zoological Parks* and Aquariums, 4550 Montgomery Ave., Suite 940 N, Bethesda, MD 20814. You can post the fact sheet and photo of your animal in the school office and share, with pride, the animal you are helping.

Conservation
Projects

Compost "Construction"

Commercial fertilizers are produced by biogeochemical methods that create environmental problems. Learn how to produce *compost*-an organic fertilizer made from a mixture of dead plant and animal materials. Mix fruit and vegetable peelings, eggshells, coffee grounds, tea leaves and tea bags, bones and shellfish parts together in a large plastic bin. Turn the mixture over every once in a while. Explain that, over time, these materials will break down and become rich fertilizer for gardens and farms.

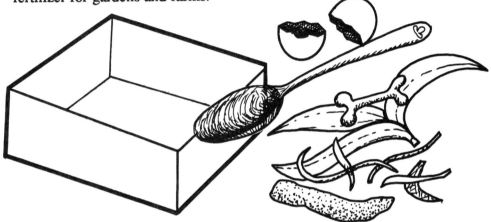

Classroom Conservation

Brainstorm a list of ways to *conserve*. For example, pack lunches in reusable cloth bags (you could even make them in class) instead of brown bags, clean up with rags instead of paper towels, turn off lights when leaving the room or use water-based paints and markers for art projects. From the list, choose four (or more) ways your class can conserve **at school**. Remind each other daily–you are making a difference!

Set up a recycling center in your classroom. Prepare several large, sturdy cardboard boxes or bins to collect the glass, plastic and paper. Label each box with what kind of material goes into it. Ask parents to help take the materials to the community recycling center. Remember to take the caps or lids off jars and bottles before putting them in the box.

Wildlife Friends

Make a mural showing some of the world's endangered species, dolphins, panda bears, rhinoceros, African elephants, jaguars and bald eagles to name a few.

Be kind to bugs and spiders. They play an important role in the animal food chain.

Project Planner

Make Room for Maps

Start a collection of maps to use in a variety of projects.

ASK KIDS TO JOIN IN by bringing maps from home. If a neighbor takes a business trip to another city, ask him to bring back a map. If a family goes on vacation, bring back a map!

START A LETTER CAMPAIGN to Chambers of Commerce and worldwide travel bureaus requesting free maps of cities, states, provinces and countries.

VISIT YOUR LOCAL city hall and obtain maps of your community.

CHECK YOUR NEWSPAPER for weather maps, political maps and world event maps. Cut out and laminate for future projects.

LOOK THROUGH MAGAZINES for maps to events, travel destintions and article locations. Cut out and laminate for future projects.

ARIZONA

Don't leave a stone unturned!
Consider these map possibilities ...

- Shopping mall directories
- Historical landmarks and routes
- National parks
- Parade routes
- Theme parks, zoos
- Product manufacuturing and agricultural maps
- Bicycle and backpacking trails
- Campgrounds

As maps are added, ideas for new projects will be born. Be sure to cover the map basics with students.

Learn about the *kind* of information found on maps.
Look for keys and legends and learn how to use them.
Become familiar with maps that show enlargements of small areas.
Calculate scale.
Find directional symbols.

Make Room for Maps

Integrate maps into your curriculum for some exciting, hands-on learning. As maps are added to your classroom collection, ideas for new projects and investigations will be born.

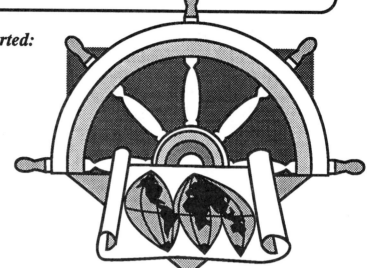

Here are some ideas to get you started:

- **Imagine** you're a tour guide and use a map of historical landmarks to plan a day for your customers. Map your route.

- **Use the scale** to measure and calculate distances from one location another.

- **Write** to a "visiting relative" and give them directions to your city.

- **Take a walking field trip** around your community. Determine what direction you are heading.

- **Compare** weather conditions around the state or province, the country, the world.

- **Pretend** you are a television parade commentator. Describe the parade route.

- **Hunt** through the newspaper; then locate article locations.

- **Make** a chart listing national monuments or geographic features and where to find them.

- **Categorize** the shops in a mall—make a listing of restaurants, specialty shops, sporting goods stores etc.

- **Assign** research projects creatively. "Close your eyes and pick a map…Close your eyes and point to a spot on the map…"

- **Compile** a list of countries. Know their location.

- **Play** a game of "HUNT AND FIND". Divide into groups, use the same maps and have a contest to see which team can find the location first.

- **Plan** your "trip" to the zoo or entertainment park. Make a list of what you want to see and put them in a logical visiting order according to the map.

- **List** the geographic features in a particular area.

- **Find** an *unusually-named* city. Write an imaginary story about it.

Group Effort

Cooperative Learning
FUNDAMENTALS

*Cooperative learning extends the meaning of "teacher" as students, working and interacting in small groups, learn from one another. Use these ideas and strategies to make cooperative learning work successfully in every classroom — **your** classroom.*

SUPPORT

Group members must be supportive. They need to help, listen to, and be happy for each other. Being able to count on one another is important!

INTERDEPENDENCE

The group's efforts and work as a whole are as important as each individual's. If a spelling group has six students and two are having difficulty, the other four members should pitch in and help. The goal is group success and achievement. Group members should feel comfortable about asking others for help.

ACCOUNTABILITY

Every student in a group is responsible for learning new material and completing his assignment. A student with poor work habits cannot depend on the others in the group to "carry him". Similarly, a strong student should not offer to do most of the work. Members must share in the responsibilities and be accountable for their contribution to the group effort.

TEACHING REMINDERS

Monitor the work and behavior of your groups on a daily basis. Check to be sure that each student is working cooperatively. Resolve group problems before they get too big.

Guide students in the necessary skills—social and academic. Point out individual strengths and show them how to put these strengths to use in a group situation.

Provide for a variety of cooperative learning situations. Reading, math and spelling groups are implemented daily. Also create groups for one-time situations such as recreational teams (softball, classroom games), special projects (reports, investigations), creative efforts (art, music), and task-oriented (recycling project, clean-up campaign).

A Class Divided

Here are some innovative ways to divide into cooperative learning groups.

BY HEIGHT...

Line up tallest to shortest. To create groups of four, for example, take the first two and last two in line.

BY CLOTHING...

Shoe type–Velcro, laces, slip ons, loafers...
Color–all those wearing green ...
Shirt–all those wearing t-shirts...sweatshirts...

BY PHYSICAL FEATURES...

Hair color...length...
Eye color

BY NAMES...

Number of syllables in last name
Middle initials
Letters in last name

BY PERSONAL INFORMATION...

Birthdays–by month, date
Favorites–
    if your favorite *color* is red...blue...
    if your favorite *cookie* is chocolate chip...oatmeal...
    if your favorite *ice cream* is chocolate...strawberry...
Interests–if you like to play baseball...collect stamps...
Lunch–if you have potato chips in your lunch...ham sandwich...

BY LOTTERY...

Color–if you pick the red paper...green paper...
Items–toothpicks...buttons...
Sticks–pre-paint popsicle sticks, divide by color

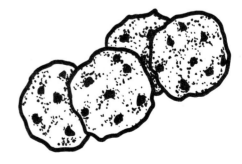

Group Effort

Interior Decorators

> *"Hire" your students as interior decorators. Divide into groups of four to six children who will work together to plan and decorate a classroom center.*

Ask them to decide on the following for their center project:
- a theme
- furnishings
- decorations and color scheme
- supplies

Then discuss and delegate responsibilities for carrying out the plan.

Here are some suggestions for the "newly employed" classroom decorators:

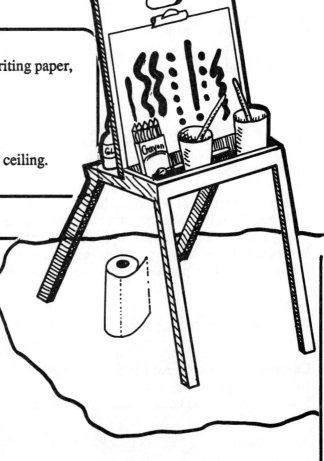

Writing Center

Stock with pencils, rubber stamps and pads, writing paper, stationery and envelopes (donated by parents).

Include a writing storage file for each student.

Hang brightly colored stuffed pencils from the ceiling.

Art Center

Provide crayons, colored pencils, markers, construction paper scraps, glue, scissors, watercolors, paintbrushes, art paper and paper towels, for cleanup.

Set up an easel. Cover the floor with plastic sheeting.

Create artist palettes to adorn the walls around the center.

Snack Center

Stock with a popcorn popper, plastic spoons, forks and knives.

Ask for donated food items. Boxes of crackers and cereal and bags of pretzels and raisins can be combined together to make nutritious and tasty treats.

Discover the chefs in your classroom! Attendance at this center is strictly controlled!

Fitness Center

Include exercise mats, books about fitness and exercise, bean bag weights.

Magazine Center

Ask classmates to contribute favorite magazines from home. Encourage the sharing of pictures and articles.

Fill the center with inviting pillows and low bookshelves stocked with all kinds of interesting magazines.

But the best ideas will come from the students! Your room will, no doubt, be filled with the most imaginative centers ever

...and the kids will love visiting them!

Group Effort

Plan a Special Day

Involve children in planning and implementing motivational theme days to take place during the school year just when everyone "needs a change of pace". The degree of student involvement will, of course, depend on the age of your students. But they ALL can be involved in some way!

1. Before you begin...

Brainstorm as a class. List some events you have attended—birthday parties, concerts, circus, park play days, community functions. Talk about the planning and organization involved.

Discuss the concept of a "THEME". Give examples of how that theme can "tie" into classroom activities in *all* subject areas.

Plan a day *together*. List the things they need to plan:

activities and projects	schedule
materials needed	refreshments
program, invitation (if there will be guests)	

Evaluate the day you planned. Are the activities well-rounded. Were any details missed?

2. Divide into groups...

... with the objective that each group will plan a special day.(The number of groups will depend on the number of theme days you would like to have during the school year.) Provide them with a copy of these pages, (following):

SPECIAL DAY SPRINGBOARDS
THEME DAY PLANNING GUIDE

Meet with each group as they make their plans. Help them evaluate their progress.

Review the final plans. Do they need to add anything?

Schedule the special days in your yearly calendar.

3. Before the Big Day...

Meet with each group and assign the jobs that need to be accomplished.

Check to see that all necessary materials have been assembled, all guests or speakers (if any) have been invited and confirmed, all films or additional resources have been ordered.

4. On the Big Day!...

Ask group members to serve as hosts. Let them pass out materials and help with preparations.

Recognize and reward each member efforts toward a successful and exciting day!

Special Day Planning Page

Use this as a guide for planning your special day. Add more paper if there is not enough room here to complete your plans.

Group Members

Theme

Activities and Projects

Schedule

Materials

Refreshments

Special Day Springboards

Solar System Adventure

Star Search

Ice Cream Frenzy

Sports Day

Dinosaur Day

A Pirate's Life for Me

Something Magical

Jelly Bean Jamboree

Invention Convention

Ocean Voyage

Desert Caravan

Hobby Fest

Around our Town

Ants and Plants

Something GIANT

Indian Pow-Wow

Whales and Snails

Things with Wings

Bugs and Butterflies

Under the Big Top

Time Machine Travel

The End of the Rainbow

Color Carnival

Castles and Dragons

Animal Adventure

Under the Sea

Backwards Day

Strings and Things

Cowboys and Campfires

Imagination Day

Fairy Tale Fun

Monsters and More

Holiday Themes

Haunted Classroom

Turkey Time

Winter Wonders

Cupid's Adventures

EGGciting Adventures

Santa's Workshop

New Year's Celebration

Fun and Fireworks

Tree Time

Spring Fling

School Supermarket

Here's a hands-on categorizing activity students can enjoy in groups.

Ask students to bring in empty food containers—cans (with labels on!) and boxes (cereal, crackers, cake mixes, spaghetti), milk cartons. Collect a wide variety and then divide the class into 4-5 groups with about 6 students per group. This group activity coordinates well with "Shop and Sort" and "Reorganize the Refrigerator" in the student section of "Let's Get Organized."

Give each group an assortment of "food items" to categorize. See how each group organizes their collection. Students should be ready to explain how their group approached the activity.

◆ Did different students in each group have different suggestions?

◆ Why was one suggestion used over another?

◆ Is one way more efficient than another or is it just a matter of individual preference?

◆ What were the different ways the groups categorized the "food items?" (alphabetically, by food type, by size of the container, refrigerator foods vs. pantry foods, etc.)

Think about it

Allow students to share any unusual ways foods may be organized in their homes for special reasons (food on low shelves for young children to reach, etc.)

Group Effort

Cereal Box
Scrutiny

Why do people love to read cereal boxes? Cereal boxes are covered with colorful and interesting information—games, recipes, nutritional content, send-away certificates, and funny characters . Incorporate the information on these boxes into some dynamic activities.

Divide the class into four groups. Assign each group a different task as described below. (Decide which four are best suited for *your* students.) Turn them loose to "explore" the cereal box information and prepare their final reports.

INGREDIENT INVESTIGATORS

What are the most common ingredients in cereal? Which cereals have the highest nutritional content?
> Chart the results.
> Conduct a "mini" *taste test*.
Do nutrition and appealing taste go together?

GAME GETTERS

Cut out any games found on the cereal boxes. Laminate them and set up a "CEREAL BOX GAME CENTER" for classmates to enjoy. Be sure to provide all necessary materials.

RECIPE READERS

Cut out *or* copy recipes off the box. File them on index cards in a recipe box. Make the recipes available for children to copy, take home and prepare for class sampling. The group should decide on ONE recipe to prepare and serve their classmates.

FREEBIE FINDERS

Cut out coupons, and send away for items offered for FREE with "proof of purchase" or other requirement. Make a poster showing the things you sent for. Use the freebies that you receive as student awards and prizes.

GRAPH GANG

Choose 6 to 8 types of cereal and use them to gather statistics on student "favorites". Make a large bar graph. Cut off the box fronts to label each column. Record student favorites and report on the results.

Cereal Box
Scrutiny

When the investigating is over and the reports presented, recycle any leftover cereal boxes! They shouldn't go to waste.Put them to use for creating . . .

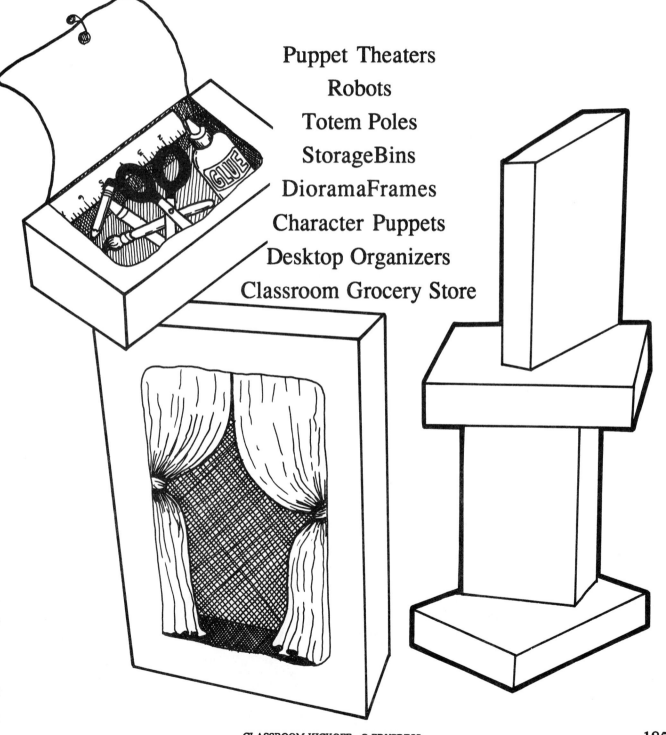

Puppet Theaters
Robots
Totem Poles
StorageBins
DioramaFrames
Character Puppets
Desktop Organizers
Classroom Grocery Store

Paper Folding

> *This creative activity will bring out the artist in every student as it involves easy, fun and colorful designing techniques.*

Prior to introducing the sculpture part of the activity, demonstrate different ways to give paper dimension. Provide a few pieces of paper and scissors to each student so they can practice as you demonstrate each technique.

Folding:

Fan-fold/accordion-fold:

Overlap-folding:
Take two strips of paper and staple or paste corners together at a right angle. Fold one strip over the other as shown in illustration.

Continue until you reach the end of each strip and staple to hold.

These make super legs for puppets, pumpkin people, etc.

Fringing: Use a wide strip of paper and cut long or short cuts for assorted effects. Also try curling the ends around a pencil to add dimension.

Paper Folding

Curling: Cut paper in strips. Roll each strip around a pencil, a tube, a dowel, a crayon or other tube-shaped object. Pull paper from object. Use different thicknesses to roll paper around for a variety of sizes.

Spiraling: Cut a circle. Start at outer edge and continue cutting in towards the center. Large circles produce long spirals; small circles produce short spirals.

Crunching: An easy technique that gives bulk and texture to the sculpture design— students crunch paper with their hands.

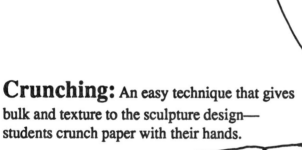

Twisting: Create a long, thin strip of paper similar to confetti curls. Wind into a continuous, concentric ring; then unwind and pull.

When students know these paper techniques, continue with the second part of the lesson: **A GROUP PAPER SCULPTURE!**

Paper Sculpture

Note: Practice PAPER FOLDING techniques (previous page) prior to beginning this project.

Preparation: Have on hand a wide variety of types of colored papers: construction paper, giftwrap, foils, newspaper, colored tissue paper, wallpaper, specialty papers from your art supplies and others brought in by your students.

Divide your class into groups of 4-5 students. Provide a mix of your artistic students as well as unartistic students within each group. Allow each child in the group to select from the paper choices. As a rule, two choices per student gives a good variety for a working group of 4-5 students. Advise students that their **individual** choices will become part of the group work; therefore students should coordinate with each other so there is a variety within the group.

Provide a piece of tagboard or heavy cardboard (approximately 18 x 24) for the backing board. Students may choose to color this, paint it or cover it with decorative paper.

Using the techniques of curling, folding, spiraling, fringing, crunching and twisting (plus other student-inspired techniques) give your young "Rodins" free reign to decorate and create a 3-dimensional paper sculpture.

Students should arrange their sculpture several ways before pasting or stapling their final choice into place.

Display prominently for a bright, eye-appealing arty room!

Book Swap

> *Involve your students in a book swap meet! Recycle books, stimulate reading and expose children to the variety of books all at the same time! Here's how to organize a successful swap.*

- **Send home a notice** explaining the project. Ask for books children can trade or swap with their classmates. Parents must initial the inside front cover as their consent that each book has been approved for the swap meet. Encourage all students to bring at least one book. You may want to set a maximum number a child may contribute.

- **Set a goal** of perhaps 75-100 books for the class.

- **Select a day** for the big event. Mark your calendars!

- **On the day** of the swap meet, the trading may be handled in one of two ways:

1. INDIVIDUAL DISPLAY

Each student creates a desktop display of the books they wish to swap. They may write a clever banner slogan to promote each book.

Several students at a time take turns walking around with their books to swap. When they return to their seats, they display only the books they brought from home, not the new ones swapped.

2. GROUP DISPLAY

Give each child a ticket for every book contributed to the swap.

Display all books on a large table. Children may work beforehand to organize the books—by author, subject, fiction or non-fiction—for the table display.

Students take a trip to the table to swap their ticket for a "new" book of their choosing. If they do not wish to use all their tickets they may put them in a pile for other students.

If any books are left when the swap meet is over, invite another class to select books *or* donate them to a local hospital or children's home.

Group Effort

Pizza, Please!

Whet your students' appetites with this fun and innovative paper pizza project!

Divide students into groups of 4-5. Supply each group with pieces of construction paper to reflect colors in a pizza—yellow for the crust, red for the sauce, brown for pepperoni, white for cheese, green for pepper, etc. String and yarn add interesting texture. Crumpled tissue makes super sausage!

Ask each group to design a pizza using paper, scissors, paste, string, yarn and their imaginations. Encourage creativity! Let each group decide on the size, shape, and ingredients they want.

Students may ask for additional materials—the same supplies should be available to all groups.

Once the concept is explained, let your students loose to produce their paper pizzas. Have each group sign the back with their names. Display the finished artwork on your bulletin board.

The class may vote to award "blue ribbons" to the winners in each pizza category:

- Most colorful
- Tastiest looking
- Most unusual ingredients
- Funniest
- Best use of materials

Group Effort

Amazing Murals

Encourage group effort through this bulletin board activity.

Divide a board into segments—vertical, horizontal or freeform. Use colored yarn or colored construction paper and eye-appealing lettering to separate the sections.

Select a topic you are currently studying or a season as the theme and then divide the bulletin board into various parts for students to illustrate.

Students should work cooperatively in groups discussing each student's contribution to the group effort before work begins.

Group Effort

Beginning to Broadcast

As an introduction to this activity, ask your students to view and become familiar with the morning or evening news shows on television. Who are the key people that are seen? What are their specific roles? What kind of information does each report?

Divide into groups of 6-student news teams. Each group will decide among themselves who will be:

- **anchorman** or **anchorwoman**
- **national** news reporter
- **local** news reporter
- **world** news reporter
- **state** news reporter
- **weather** reporter

Responsibilities of the group include:

- **reading** the newspaper, listening to the news on the radio or television and becoming familiar with the news of the day they will will report on.

- **writing** a brief summary of the story they will report in an appealing way for reporting to the class.

- **practicing** the written copy before 'broadcasting' to the class.

- **completing** the **NEWS ASSIGNMENTS** information sheet.

Students may choose to have an anchor 'team' of two people and have an informal news show or may opt for a more formal presentation of the news. Allow the group to set their own style.

Additionally, each member of the group should:

- **Bring** supporting news articles from the newspaper or news magazines and display them on the bulletin board noting the date.

- **Be ready** to point out the places on a large map to show where events have occurred and the locations of high and low temperatures.

Select a different group each Monday and allow them adequate preparation time. You'll enjoy the varied approaches.

Beginning to Broadcast

Complete the information as decisions are made in your group.
Give the completed page to your teacher.

NEWS ASSIGNMENTS

News Team Members —— Assignment

1._____ Anchor Person

2._____ Local News Reporter

3._____ State News Reporter

4._____ National News Reporter

5._____ World News Reporter

6._____ Weather Person

List resources:

(Names of newspapers or magazines, television newscasts, radio stations)

1. _____ 4. _____

2. _____ 5. _____

3. _____ 6. _____

Date of "broadcast" _____

Start the Writing Process

The sooner you involve children with written language the more relaxed they will become using this form of expression. Encourage them to write freely, without worry about spelling and punctuation. Editing, if any, can be done later.

"Listing" is a good way to break the writing "ice". Experiment with the topics below; then move on to the other suggestions.

List the things...

...in your notebook
...in your classroom
...on the playground
...on the teacher's desk
...in your lunchbox

...on the schoolbus
...you saw on the way to school
...you had for breakfast
...in your desk
...you are wearing

List descriptive words for each of the above.
For example: schoolbus—yellow, noisy, crowded, loud

It's Just Routine

Try your hand at schedule writing. Work together to write the school day's schedule.

On your own, write the schedule for...
   ...your morning routine
   ...your after-school routine
   ...your evening routine

Now use your imagination and write a schedule for what you think would be a perfect weekend.

You Are in Charge

Have you ever wondered what famous people do all day?
Write a work-day schedule for:
   ...the president or prime minister of your country
   ...an astronaut
   ...a television star (anyone in particular?)
   ...a rock star

Relay Writing

> *Combine the fun of a relay race with a quick writing activity to encourage competition and sentence-writing practice.*

1. Divide your class into 4-5 teams. Try to have the same number of students in each team.

2. Make the same number of columns on your board as you have number of teams. Write sample words as shown below (or choose words of your own) to start a sentence for each team.

Last	My	Someday	When	One
night we played two games.	sister won the dance contest.	we will visit my uncle.	will we be going there?	of the cats was sick.

3. Students form a line for each team. At the "GO" signal, the first in each line races to the board and writes a word that will continue the sentence. As soon as this student adds a word, he runs back to tag the next student who then races to the board, adds a word and so on. The first team to complete a sentence wins.

TIPS

- Teams must complete a sentence with a predetermined number of words. Adapt this to your students' abilities.

- You may want to have *more* teams with *fewer* students giving each child more chances to participate.

- Consider requiring that only sentences with correct spelling can qualify as winning team.

- Award winning teams some small perk: selecting a game at P.E., etc.

Silly School Stuff

Write about these silly school happenings...

...the day there was no teacher

...the day a snake got loose in the classroom

...the day a dinosaur came to school

...the day you forgot your name

...the day you got stuck in the bathroom

...the day *you* were the teacher

...the day Frankenstein was the principal

...the day everyone forgot their lunch

...the day you only had pickles for lunch

...the day a spaceship landed on the playground

...the day you brought a pet to school

...the day your teacher turned into a frog

...the day your teacher turned into an elephant

...the day you switched identities with your best friend

...the day the schoolbus was an airplane

...the day you took a field trip to Mars

...the day there was a mummy in the coat closet

...the day the classroom was carpeted with marshmallows

Help. I'm in the closet.

Here are some more writing topics to kick off a new school year.

Time Machine Travel

You've been granted the ability to travel forward in time during the school year. Write about...

- ...what month it is
- ...any special day
- ...what you are doing
- ...who you are with

Now you've been granted the ability to travel back in time to relive a special day in your *life*. Write about...

- ...when the day was
- ...what you were doing
- ...who you were with
- ...why you want to relive it

Two To the Teacher

You can tell only two things to your teacher about each of the following. So think carefully of two special and important things about...

- ...yourself
- ...your family
- ...where you live
- ...what you enjoy doing
- ...what you care about
- ...what you don't like

Describe the perfect

classroom
school day
school lunch
teacher
friend
student
school playground
school

THE GENIE GRANTS MY WISHES

My life has changed since the day I met the genie. That's because he granted me two wishes. I'll tell you about them.

_____

_____

_____

_____

_____

_____

_____

_____

_____

The Monster That Ate My Homework

I know you'll find this hard to believe, but one day while I was on my way to school _____

_____

_____

_____

_____

_____

_____

Draw a picture on the back of the paper of the monster that ate your homework.

Cut and Paste a Story

> *Children learn to "build" a story by using the story pictures on the following pages. Proceed through the different levels described below and watch their story-telling abilities grow.*
>
> **Teacher Preparation:** Reproduce the selected "Cut and Paste" story board for each student. Provide scissors, paste and a large sheet of white construction paper. (Level one requires only scissors.)
>
> **Student Preparation:** Cut apart the pictures on the dotted line. Color each picture. (This helps familiarize them with the content of each.)

Level One:

Create a story *for* the children. As the story progresses, they find the corresponding picture from the scrambled group of pictures on their desk and move them into position, left to right on their desktop. When the story is finished ask the children to help give the story a title. This provides a chance to summarize the story and pull out some main ideas.

Then scramble the pictures and create a group story. You may need to help them with a title or an opening sentence. Repeat the procedure of moving the pictures into sequential position but this time the students take turns contributing sentences to "write" a story.

One snowy night I heard a
knock on my door...

Level Two:

Describe a *rebus* story to the children. Show them how to write a story by pasting the pictures into sequential position and adding a word or two between. Ask students to take turns telling their rebus story to a classmate.

Cut and Paste a Story

Level Three:

Work *individually,* arrange and paste the pictures in story order.* Write simple sentences to create a story. As skills progress, write a more complete story, adding details and descriptions.

*To display the stories, provide colored construction paper. Fold the paper in half. Paste the pictures to the left half and the story to the right.

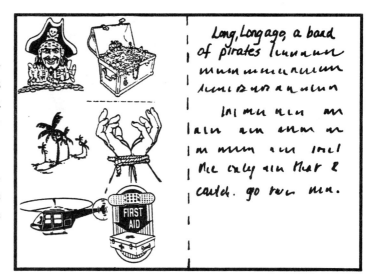

OPTIONAL:

"Cut and Paste" Story Center

After the children have progressed through the different cut and paste story levels, they'll be ready to tackle more on their own. Create a classroom **"CUT AND PASTE"** story center.

1. To make story starters, cut out magazine pictures, glue them to index cards, laminate and put them in numbered envelopes. Number pictures to correspond with envelope number for easy cleanup and organization. Students can contribute to this preparation.

2. Provide each student with a folder.

3. At the center, students select an envelope, look at the pictures and write a story. (There is no pasting involved. Be sure each story is numbered to correspond to the envelope.)

4. Students store each finished story in their folder. (This gives you a chance to evaluate each students writing progress.)

Center Tips:

Let them know their stories will not be corrected for punctuation or spelling. This is strictly a creativity center!

During free moments, pull stories of the same number to read to the class. They will be amazed at the variety of plots, characters and twists the created from the same pictures!

Cut and Paste a Story

Write Right Away

Send students spinning and make any writing activity silly and special! Use this format to add zest to letter writing, story writing, sentence or paragraph development practice.

IT'S EASY!

Reproduce a supply of the round-writing circle (following) to have on hand for any assignment. Students write their work in concentric circles starting at the outer edge and going inward.

Encourage children to write neatly!

When writing is completed, use a brad through the center of each circle and attach it to a colorful square of construction paper.

Then just turn the wheel and read!

You may want to feature the writing on a bulletin board headed:

ROUND WRITING
or
ALL-AROUND WRITING
or even
ROUND AND ROUND WE GO!

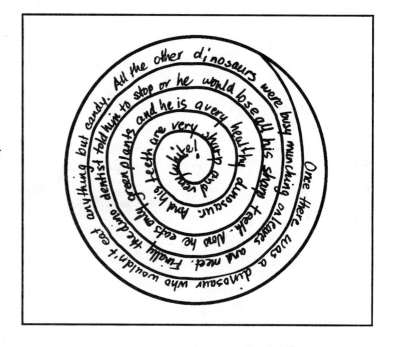

Encourage students and classroom visitors to "take a spin" at the story board!

Try these RRRRound RRRRwriting activities:

RED WRITING—write with red pen, pencil, marker or crayon. Great for Valentine's Day stories!

RED WRITING HOOD— Rewrite the beginning, middle or end of a fairy tale.

ROVER WRITING—Write a letter to—or a story about—your dog or pet.

ROUND Writing
Circle Pattern

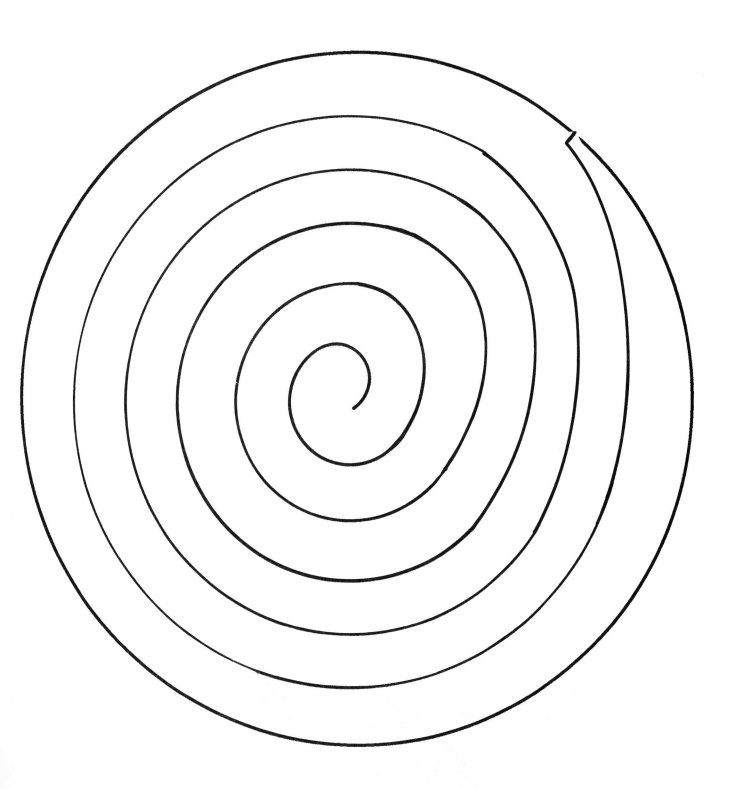

Colorful Rhymes

Here's a simple and creative writing exercise where students write—and the class shares—short, colorful rhymes.

First Line: Write a question about a color.

What is white?

Second Line: Students answer with something that everyone can picture as that color.

A cloud is white.

Last Line: Add a line that rhymes with the color.

What is white?
A cloud is white.
In the sky so bright.

Here are some other color rhymes to share with students to get them going:

What is gold?
My ring is gold.
It's beautiful and old.

What is green?
A leaf is green.
In fall they're a pretty
scene.

Ask students to write their own color rhymes. It may be helpful to brainstorm a list of color-related words before they begin.

What is...

red? (berries, bricks, the flag)
green? (a leaf, grass)
blue? (the sea, the sky, someone's eyes)
yellow? (corn, butter, the sun)
pink? (cotton candy, a baby girl, a rose)
brown? (someone's hair, a dog)

Display student rhymes on a colorful bulletin board. Back each color rhyme with paper to highlight that color. Students will enjoy writing short rhymes and being creative about the use of colors.

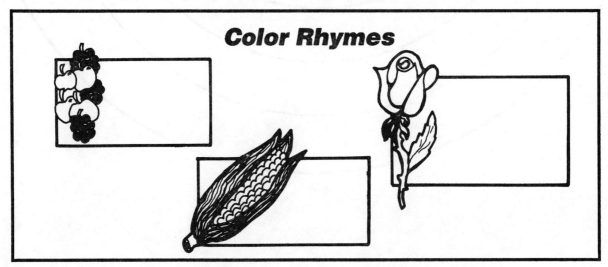

Color Rhymes

RIDDLE WRITING
Here's some riddle-writing fun!

Share these riddles with your students. Ask them to guess the answer.
Then discuss what made the riddle easy–or difficult–to figure out.

RIDDLE ONE

My shape is long and thin and my color is creamy. I come in a package
with a lot of other creamy, long, thin pieces, just like me. Put me in a pot
of hot, boiling water—OUCH!—and I get soft and bend easily. Then I
get rinsed and covered with sauce.

What am I?   *(spaghetti)*

RIDDLE TWO

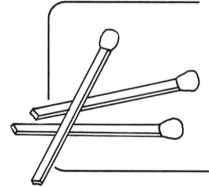

I am small, narrow and made of wood. Usually my tip is red and
the rest of me the color of light wood. If you rub my tip against
a hard, rough brown strip, I burst into an orange flame.

What am I?   *(match)*

Practice writing riddles together. Start by describing a **Jack o' Lantern**. This lends
itself to colorful phrases that will be relatively easy for students to write. For addition practice
as a group try writing riddles for

eyeglasses   button   star   lemon   kite

When students are ready, ask them to write riddles of their own.

Set aside some Riddle-reading time for children to share their riddle with the class and
let them guess the answer.

Let's Talk
Strategies for Open Communication

Set the tone for open communication in your class by introducing a variety of easy and comfortable ways students can talk with you and with their classmates in a positive, informal manner.

It's Our Secret

Establish an **"It's Our Secret"** approach where students can arrange to talk with you about a personal or school problem in confidence. You may want to have a sign-up sheet or an appointment book where students can sign up for private time.

Just Talking

Meet with a small group or meet with individual students for lunch 'just to talk' to get to know each other one-on-one—away from classroom distractions.

Kindness Corner

Set up a "Kindness Corner" where students can go to help one another and communicate in a positive way. Establish rules for its use.

Read to Me

During reading time, set up a schedule where students can come to read to you personally, away from the rest of the group. This will give you the opportunity to check on oral reading and comprehension and talk informally about the book.

Air It Out

Spend some of your off-duty recess minutes outdoors chatting with your students or playing a game with them.

Let's Whisper

Set up a "Whisper Time" when students can talk softly to their classmates. You may want to establish rules for talking only with students close by or you may permit walking around for whisper time. Set a time limit of perhaps 5-7 minutes. No secrets!

It's My Turn

Set up a regular time for an "Open Forum" where students can 'speak their minds' to get things off their chest. This time should focus on issues and opinions. A student might like to make it known that it really bothers him when people attempt to smoke in a non-smoking area. Discussions and debates may arise from student opinions. This time, however, should not be judgemental—children should be free to air their views without fear of being wrong or off-base.

CLASSROOM KICKOFF • © EDUPRESS

People Picnic

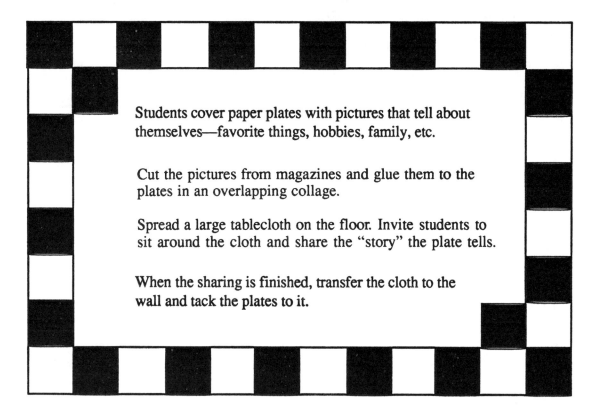

Students cover paper plates with pictures that tell about themselves—favorite things, hobbies, family, etc.

Cut the pictures from magazines and glue them to the plates in an overlapping collage.

Spread a large tablecloth on the floor. Invite students to sit around the cloth and share the "story" the plate tells.

When the sharing is finished, transfer the cloth to the wall and tack the plates to it.

TONGUE TWISTERS

> *Tongue twisters are guaranteed to get you laughing…but that's not all. They also provide some super lessons in rhyming, alliteration and concentration!*

Here are some tongue twisters to start with. Practice them as a group. Then divide into pairs for some "one on one" practice. Pairs can keep track of how many times a partner says the twister correctly—or just have some fun with a new friend.

Sixty-six sick chicks.

A noise annoys an oyster.

I see icy icicles.

Good blood, bad blood.

Rubber baby buggy bumpers.

The sun shines on the shop signs.

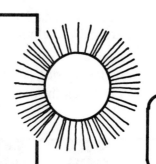

Frank threw Fred Three free throws.

Greek grape leaves.

Double bubble gum bubbles double.

Betty bought a bit of butter to make her batter better.

A big black bug bit a big black bear.

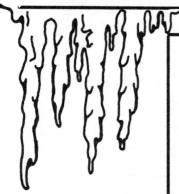

Slick super-sleuths.

Wise ones want wishes.

My big black bear bled blood.

Peter Piper picked a peck of pickled peppers.

Timed Talks

*To encourage speaking before a group, use this exercise as an ice-breaker. Children must speak for only a short **timed** amount—1, 2 or 3 minutes. Use a timer or hourglass to keep children to the limit.*

Start with quickie "one-minute talks". As a motivator, place small folded pieces of paper, on which topics have been written, in a box or paper bag. Student reaches in, pulls out a paper and talks about that topic for the selected amount of time. The topics should be ones that **every** student can talk about.

Some suggestions to get you started:

● a funny thing someone in my family does

● all about my favorite food

● a good movie I've seen

● what I like to share

● what makes me feel good

● something I hate to do

● my favorite TV show

● a scary thing that happened to me

● something nice someone did for me

● the perfect 'fun' day

Another approach is to assign a topic the night before and give students time to plan their talk. Encourage children to practice at home so they can get the important points said within the allotted time.

Sixty Second Solutions

Problem solving is an important life skill. Spend spare moments between subjects, after clean up and before recess discussing problems and their solutions.

As children become practiced in the problem-solving process they become more independent thinkers. And that leads to students who don't turn to the teacher for the solution to every problem or question that confronts them.

Problem solving topics are suggested on this and the following page. Children can contribute to the topics by mentioning a problem they have faced. They will probably be surprised to find fellow classmates who have had the same problem.

Problem Solving Steps

1. What is the problem?
2. What are the alternative solutions?
3. What are the consequences of each solution?

 You saw money fall out of a classmate's pocket. He doesn't know it fell out. No one else has seen it but you. What should you do?

You have a new classmate who doesn't speak English. How will you help him or her feel welcome in class and on the playground?

Your pet followed you to school this morning. It's almost time for school to start and you'll be late if you take your pet home. What will you do?

Your parents gave you a key to let yourself into the house when you get home. You lost the key. What will you do?

Let's Talk

Sixty Second Solutions

🕐 You are home alone and someone comes to the front door. What will you do?

🕐 You are at a large shopping center with your parents. You stop just for a moment to look in a store window an when you turn around your parents are nowhere to be seen. What will you do?

🕐 All the kids in class are talking about the exciting party a classmate has invited them to. You never got an invitation. How do you feel? What will you do?

🕐 You found an unopened candy bar on a park bench. You are really hungry! What will you do?

🕐 Your friends call you chicken because you won't do something they are doing. What will you do?

🕐 Your parents are picking you up from school but they are already ten minutes late. What should you do?

🕐 You are standing in line and someone pushes you. What will you do?

🕐 Your best friend told you that he took something from a classmate. He asks you to keep it a secret. What should you do?

🕐 You're walking to school and you're late. You've already been late three times this week! Someone stops and offers you a ride to school. What will you do?

🕐 School's over for the day. The bus leaves and after a while you realize you got on the wrong bus. What will you do?

🕐 You got in trouble on the playground for something you didn't do. What will you do?

🕐 A classmate keeps picking on you and calling you names. What will you do?

Good nutrition is always an important subject to talk about. Here are some ideas to help get the discussion started based on an important event of any school day...

...Lunch Time!

It's in the Bag

Ask students to name two things in their lunch that are good for them. Categorize their lunch items into food groups. Look at the cafeteria menu for the day. Identify the food groups recommended. Are the meals balanced?

Meal Planners

Tired of those same old school cafeteria lunches? As a class, plan several alternative lunch menus. Be sure they are balanced meals. Discuss foods that are high in cholesterol and sugar. Submit the menu plans to the nutritionist responsible for planning school lunches. Who knows? Maybe you'll see your choices on the monthly menu!

Handwiches

Here's a quick game to play that will get students thinking about good food!

Divide into groups of two or more. The first player puts his hand, palm down, on a table top, and names a sandwich ingredient. The next player covers the first player's hand with his palm and says a different sandwich ingredient. Play continues clockwise until players have both hands in the stack. Then the first player pulls out his hand, places it on top of the hand stack and begins all over again.

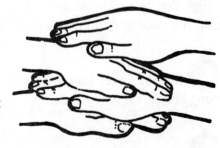

Try the game with breakfast, lunch, and dinner foods, too.

Boning Up

Use the pattern to cut a bone for each student.

Talk about the expression "bone up on" and its meaning—*gathering more information.*

Ask students to write (or dictate) something, some place or someone they would like to bone up on. It might be a country, a city, a celebrity, sport, hobby or geographical location. Store the bones in a bag.

Each day, choose a bone from the bag. Read the subject.

Everyone is asked to find out one fact or interesting bit of information about the subject to share the following day.

Use the fact-sharing as a morning opener, or a spare time filler.

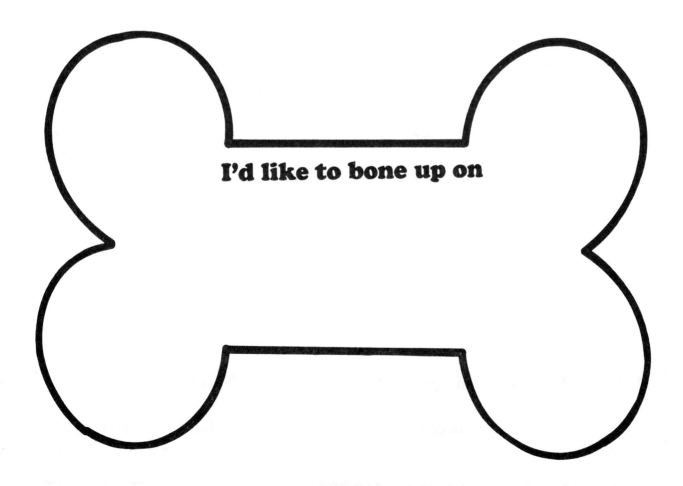

I'd like to bone up on

Partner Conversations

Pair off into partners for some fun "talking" exercises. This is not done in front of the entire class, rather, each pair finds a special place in the room where they "can talk". Stress that since half the class will be talking at the same time, quiet voices should be used.

Zip Your Lip

Pick a topic to talk about . Choose one partner to go first. At a signal from the teacher —or leader—the first person begins to talk about the topic.

At the sound of the signal again, the speaker "zips his lip" and partner begins to talk about the same topic. (The conversations do not have to be related .)

Each time the signal is heard, the speaker changes.

Some suggested topics:

* summer vacation
* a hobby
* sports
* music groups (singers)
* your dream house
* a favorite book
* a special place to visit
* fashion
* a pet

Continue On . . .

Pick a topic.

At a signal, the one of the partners begins to talk about the topic. At the signal, the speaker stops, even if it's mid-sentence, and the partner must continue the sentence and conversation about the topic. Signal often. Partners have to be good listeners!

Suggested topics:

* things you might find in a grocery store
* animals
* travel plans (a trip to a dude ranch, a ski resort)
* school lunches
* different ways to travel
* school subjects
* things that are scary
* kinds of transportation

Partner Conversations

⌐ In My Opinion ─────────────

Each partner has one minute to express a personal opinion about a statment. The partners' opinions may be the same or different. Encourage children to build the self-confidence to express their opinion and feelings about a subject. There is no right or wrong—the important lesson is that what *they* think *really* does matter.

Suggested statements:

✳ A ghost is not frightening.
✳ Playing football is dangerous.
✳ Steak is best when it is cooked rare.
✳ Mail carriers have a difficult job.
✳ It's o.k. to eat "junk food".
✳ Homework should be given every day.

───── Debates ─

Choose a topic. Partners take opposite views—even if they both have the same opinion. Each partner gets one minute to convince the other that their viewpoint is the best.

Suggested viewpoints:

✳ You should eat (should not eat) everything on your dinner plate.
✳ Boys (Girls) should be first in line.
✳ It's good (not good) to show your anger.
✳ You should always (should not always) be honest.
✳ A singing group is better than (not better than) a solo performer.
✳ Boys (girls) make the best athletes.

Role Playing

> *Involve your students in verbal communications skills as they roleplay these different scenarios. Try having students improvise the scene **without** advance planning as well as giving those students involved in the 'skit' some time to plan their scene.*

There are many benefits to incorporating role playing activities in your classroom.

Improve listening skills—participants must tune in to their role-playing partners.

Increase self-confidence—children are encouraged to express themselves openly.

Provide opportunities—students with weak writing skills have the chance to express themselves.

Develop thought process—role players must think through a problem and apply reasonable solutions.

Develop imaginations—thoughts are not slowed by the writing process.

If appropriate, children may want to raid the classroom costume box for "just the right" role-playing ensemble!

Career Topics

✦ A police officer talking to a driver who has been pulled over for going through a stop sign.

✦ A mail carrier delivering a load of holiday gifts to a lonely senior citizen.

✦ A dentist talking to a 5-year-old child on her first visit.

✦ A customer asking a salesperson for a refund because the product doesn't work.

✦ A refrigerator repair person telling an impatient customer he doesn't have the necessary part with him—and it's Friday!

✦ A garage mechanic who is late repairing a car explaining the delay to its owner.

✦ A baker trying to convince a customer to take a birthday cake decorated with the wrong name.

✦ A waitress serving free ice cream to a customer who wants chocolate cake instead.

✦ A nurse trying to calm a young boy who doesn't want the shot she is about to give.

✦ A musician talking with his conductor because he's lost his musical score for the performance.

Everyday Situations

❖ You are trying to convince your parents to let you go to a slumber party **two** nights in a row.

❖ You're shopping with your mom and you want the warm jacket **and** the red shoes. She said you can only get what you **need**. Try to convince her to buy both!

❖ It's the first time your parents have met your teacher. Introduce them to each other.

❖ You forgot to take your lunch to the bus stop. You want the bus driver to wait but he has to stay on schedule.

❖ You didn't bring a homework assignment to school. Try to convince your teacher that she should extend the due date for you.

❖ Your parents are out for the evening. You spill paint on the carpet. What will they say when they discover it and how will you handle the situation?

❖ Your bedtime is 8:00. You are trying to negotiate for an 8:30 bedtime. Talk to your mom first. Then talk to your dad.

❖ An aggressive candy salesman is at your front door. You love candy but . . .

❖ You want to trade bikes with your friend for the afternoon. Your friend is reluctant.

❖ You are babysitting your younger brother and he is not cooperating at all. You need him to brush his teeth and get ready for bed!

Fantasy

✧ Mickey Mouse asking Minnie Mouse to marry him.

✧ Donald Duck planning a vacation with Huey, Dewey and Louie.

✧ Cinderella telling her fairy Godmother she'd rather not go to the ball.

✧ "Mama Swan" trying to convince her ugly duckling that she's beautiful.

✧ The giant in Jack and the Beanstalk being friendly and helpful to Jack.

✧ A letter arrives advising your family it has won a free two-week trip to the moon.

✧ Hansel and Gretel teach their captor how to be kind and helpful.

✧ Snow White telling Grumpy (or Sleepy, or Sneezy, etc.) that she would like to adopt seven more dwarfs—all girls.

✧ The handsome prince tries to convince a very tired Sleeping Beauty to get out of bed.

Let's Talk

TELEPHONE TALK

Talking on the telephone is a skill most people use daily. Obtain as many phones as possible and provide students with an opportunity to practice some telephone skills and have some fun at the same time.

TELEPHONE SOURCES:

Contact a local telephone company for test phones you could borrow or they could donate.

Check telephone stores for discontinued or damaged phones that are being thrown away.

Ask parents to loan phones no longer in use.

The number of phones you collect will determine how you will practice phone skills. If you have only a few phones, set up a center with activity cards. With more phones, divide into small groups or pairs and conduct the practice together.

ROLEPLAYING SITUATIONS

Take turns being the caller and receiver.

DIAL 911...
Learn this important emergency procedure. What *does* happen when you dial 911? When should you use this emergency service? Practice making a call.

DIAL 411...
Practice getting a phone number from the information operator. What information will you need to provide?

MANNERS...
Practice courteous phone manners. How should the phone be answered? If the call is not for you, what should you say? If the caller is a salesperson, how will you handle it?

TELEPHONE TALK

While You were out....

Message from...

TAKE A MESSAGE...

Practice giving *and* taking phone messages.

Discuss what information should be included in a message. Practice writing and relaying a phone message to the person for whom the call was intended.

PARTY ALL 23 2:00 R.S.V.P.

BUSINESS...

Make reservations for your favorite restaurant.

Order a pizza for delivery.

Contact the police for assistance with a noisy, barking dog.

Ask your coach for practice schedules.

Take a message from your teacher, for your parents.

Call a doctor to make an appointment.

R.S.V.P. for a birthday party.

Invite a friend to spend the night with you.

Get directions to a department store.

Request homework information from a classmate.

Remind your club members about an important meeting.

Explain to your parents that you will be home late.

PROBLEMS...

Practice what to do when:

The caller is obscene.

You're home alone and someone wants to speak to an adult.

You're home along and you are frightened.

You keep getting a busy signal when you are trying to call home.

You are out and need to make an emergency call.

Pantomime Time

Sometimes, actions speak louder than words! Here is a list of good "pantomime" subjects kids will have fun trying to "act out". Use this list as a starting point. Then ask children to contribute some ideas of their own.

FACIAL EXPRESSIONS

excited
angry
sad
curious
suspicious
amazed
bored

disappointed
hurt
surprised
confused
horrified
innocent
guilty

ANIMAL ACTIONS

slithering snake
lumbering elephant
charging rhinocerous
roaring lion
restless monkey
bathing hippo
feeding giraffe

HOLIDAY AND SEASONAL

Santa coming down a chimney
Decorating a Christmas tree
Raking leaves
Dying Easter eggs
Raising a flag
Building a warm winter fire
Finding the end of the rainbow
Blown by March winds
Opening a birthday present
Involved in a snowball fight

Hanging a stocking over the fireplace
Building a snowman
Hiding Easter eggs
Cupid shooting an arrow
Planting an Arbor Day tree
Eating an ice cream cone
Caught in April showers
Sweltering under a summer sun
Lighting a menorah
Stuffing a Thanksgiving turkey

Pantomime Time

BODY MOVEMENTS

running
stretching
marching
leaping
skating
throwing
creeping
sleeping
digging
cooking

crawling
slow motion
hiking
wrestling
swimming
catching
sliding
rolling
eating
hunting

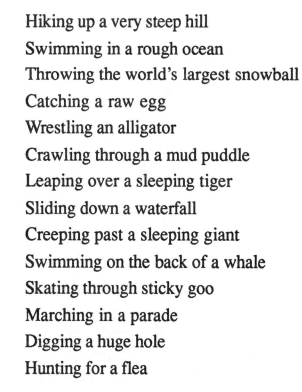

Now pantomime an imaginary event ...

Hiking up a very steep hill

Swimming in a rough ocean

Throwing the world's largest snowball

Catching a raw egg

Wrestling an alligator

Crawling through a mud puddle

Leaping over a sleeping tiger

Sliding down a waterfall

Creeping past a sleeping giant

Swimming on the back of a whale

Skating through sticky goo

Marching in a parade

Digging a huge hole

Hunting for a flea

Just Gestures

> *You don't have to speak in order to talk. This activity proves just that.*

Using **just gestures** ask students to communicate with body movements and facial expressions the following happenings.

NO WORDS OR SOUNDS OF ANY KIND CAN BE USED!

◆ I'm starving! When do we eat?
◆ Help! I can't carry this package alone.
◆ Wanna dance?
◆ I'm freezing!
◆ Can I please have my money?
◆ Where is it?
◆ Let me help you.
◆ It's in here someplace.
◆ I just want to be left alone!
◆ This is how you make a pizza.
◆ I just learned how to thread a needle!
◆ This is how you get a good suntan.
◆ I found it!!!
◆ Okay, okay! I'll walk the dog!

Try these—**USING HANDS ONLY**—no facial features or other body language.

◆ giving a manicure
◆ washing the dishes
◆ giving a haircut
◆ washing the windows
◆ trying on new rings
◆ playing the accordion
◆ opening a beautifully wrapped present
◆ using the typewriter or computer
◆ playing the violin
◆ driving a car
◆ making a phone call

Now that they've had some practice, ask students to convey some expressions or actions of their own creation. The rest of the class tries to guess.

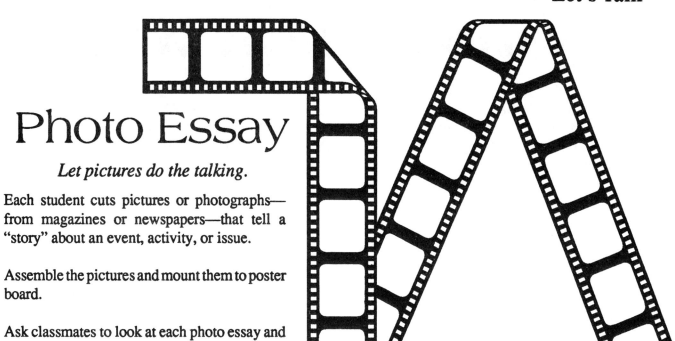

Photo Essay

Let pictures do the talking.

Each student cuts pictures or photographs—from magazines or newspapers—that tell a "story" about an event, activity, or issue.

Assemble the pictures and mount them to poster board.

Ask classmates to look at each photo essay and talk about the story they think the photo essay is trying to tell.

Introducing...THEME WEEKS

Here's a wealth of information and activities for your class, presented as THEME WEEKS—one for each month of the school year— ten in all. These weeks are intended to introduce and increase awareness of a timely topic or interesting subject. (Check the table of contents for a complete listing of themes.)

Along with resources and ideas, you'll also be given an activity for each day of the school week— Monday through Friday. The activities vary from learning a slogan or reading a book to completing a project. Use them, if you wish, as springboards for further curriculum integration and investigation.

THEME WEEKS can be planned and implemented within your class, grade level or school-wide. They can be as simple or as ambitious as you want. What is important is that the students end the week with a greater understanding of the topic.

In preparation for the week, acquaint yourself with the introductory page that presents:

Topic Summary

The objective for the week.

Words to Know

Vocabulary to incorporate into your discussions and activities. At week's end, students should have a "working knowledge" of these words. You should be hearing them use many of the words comfortably in conversation and discussion.

Community Resources

Network with community services for theme enrichment. You may want to invite a speaker to class or go on a related field trip to broaden student understanding.

References

Books pertinent to the week's theme. Look through these for added insight. Share them with your students.

Additional Ideas

Want to dig deeper? Are the students excited and want to know more? Look here for some creative suggestions.

Introducing...THEME WEEKS

Stir up some more excitement by encouraging students to participate on their own during the course of the week. You may learn more about a student's special interest by measuring their interest level during the week.

Here are some suggestions for ON YOUR OWN activities:

In the News

Children bring in newspaper or magazine articles related to the topic. Display the articles—along with the name of the special student who took the time to bring it in—on a bulletin board devoted to the theme.

Show and Tell

Students share something related to the theme...a handmade canvas grocery bag to lessen use of plastic and paper bags...a book from the family library...a related project.

My Bright Idea

Encourage students to design and share their own ideas concerning the theme. Do they have a possible solution to a problem? Have they thought of a new technique? Creative thinking, imagination and problem solving are the keys.

Sayings, Slogans & Symbols

Create timely phrases, posters and graphics to share their new-found awareness!

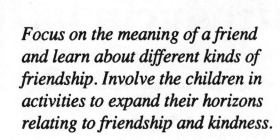

Friendship and Kindness

Topic Summary

Focus on the meaning of a friend and learn about different kinds of friendship. Involve the children in activities to expand their horizons relating to friendship and kindness.

Words to Know

friend
acquaintance
pen-pal
"best friend"
chum
playmate
buddy
neighbor
partner
UNICEF
qualities
friendship
ally

Community Resources

- **Check** with city hall to find out if your community has a "sister city". Establish a pen-pal program with a school in the sister city.

- **Visit** an animal shelter to find out about adoption or other ways you can help our animal friends.

- **Invite** a speaker to explain community service programs such as "Meals on Wheels" or "Big Brothers".

References

1. *Sweet Valley Twins* series created by Francine Pascal
   Bantam-Skylark
2. *Babysitters Club*, Ann M. Martin
   Scholastic
3. *Learning the Value of Friends*, Elaine P. Goley
4. *Making Friends*, Fred Rogers
5. *Real Friends; Becoming the Friend You'd Like ...*,
   Barbara Varenhorst

Additional Ideas

- **Choose** Secret Pals within your class. Encourage acts of kindness.
- **Find out** about countries that are friends/allies.
- **Establish** a time for students to share acts of kindness and friendship performed by their classmates.
- **Adopt** another class in the school. Make a new friend in the class.

Friendship and Kindness

Monday

Discuss the true meaning of a friend. What qualities do you look for in a friend? Are your friends similar to you or different? How do you like a friend to act towards you? Ask children to express their feelings about a "best friend" who has moved away. Share stories about special things your friend has done for you.

Tuesday

Involve the class in a kindness project by learning how UNICEF works to help underprivileged children in other countries. Brainstorm ways to express kindness and friendship towards children in a faraway land or in your own neighborhood. Collect toys or canned goods to share with the underprivileged in your community.

Wednesday

Create a multicultural friendship border of children from around the world to decorate your classroom. Arrange each drawing with hands touching, similar to a strip of cut-out paper dolls. Set up a table with books about stories of children in other lands. Listen to and learn the song "It's a Small World."

Thursday

Write a letter to a friend you haven't seen in a while. Renew the friendship. Start a letter-writing program to other friends.

Friday

Talk about life-long friends. Encourage children to speak to their parents about friends they have and how long they have had them. Are many parents still friendly with their childhood friends? Why do they think those friendships lasted? Share the information. Discuss the importance of "making new friends but keeping the old."

Safety

Topic Summary

Encourage students to develop "safety sense". Learning to think carefully and act safely can prevent injury and accidents. Knowing safety guidelines can lead to "safety sense".

Words to Know

crossing guard
safety
safety guidelines
crosswalk
poisonous
sunburn/sunscreen
hypothermia/hyperthermia
protection
pedestrian
safety sense
intersection

Community Resources

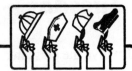

- **Talk** to the school crossing guard about the job he or she does.
- **Ask** the owner of a bicycle shop to demonstrate bicycle care and the use of a helmet.
- **Visit** a sporting goods store and have the owner show and demonstrate safety equipment.
- **Invite** a lifeguard to discuss water (and/or boating) safety.

References

1. **Children's Press Safety Series**, Dorothy Chlad. Titles include:
   Bicycles Are Fun to Ride   *Playing on the Playground*
   Poisons Make You Sick   *Riding on a Bus*
   When I Cross the Street   *When There is Fire*
2. **Safety Series from Gloucester Press**, Pete Sanders. Tites include:
   At Home
   On The Road
   Traffic Safety
3. *The Dangers of Strangers*, Carole Vogel, Dillon Press
4. **SAFETY FIRST series**, Eugene Baker. Titles include:
   Fire, Outdoor, School and Water (swimming)

Additional Ideas

Compare automobile injury statistics for passengers wearing seatbelts and those not wearing seatbelts.
Gather safety pamphlets from police and fire departments and make a safety library for students to check out and take home.
Conduct a safety inspection in your classroom.

Safety

Monday

Traffic Safety–*Head out to the playground* and mark off an intersection, complete with crosswalks and traffic signals made from colored construction paper circles. Take turns being automobiles and pedestrians. Learn when it is safe to cross the street. If there is a busy intersection near your school, take a walking-field trip there and spend some time observing traffic and signals. Discuss playing in the street by your home and the dangers of crossing the street where there is no crosswalk or signal.

Tuesday

Create a list of things to check for *safety at home:*

   Poisonous substances–Are they properly labeled and well out of reach?

   Fire prevention–Are there any overloaded electrical outlets? Are wires frayed? Do you have a working smoke detector?

Does the second floor have escape ladders in each room?

   Kitchen precautions–Are knives stored safely? Do you know not to put an electrical appliance in water? Is baking soda handy in the kitchen for grease fires?

Ask children to take the list home and report back the next day.

Wednesday

Bring a supply of clothing for various *weather* conditions. Play a weather game–describe the weather conditions and have children choose appropriate attire from the clothing supply. Discuss sunscreen and the protection of your skin in *any* weather!

Discuss the symptoms of hypothermia (shivering due to low body heat) and hyperthermia (dizziness, weakness and nausea due to high body heat). Decide what to do in each situation.

Thursday

Role play automobile safety. Ask small groups of children to demonstrate *unsafe* passenger habits and the other group to demonstrate *safe* passenger habits. (One group member should be the driver and the other the passengers.) Stress the importance of wearing seatbelts, locking doors, not distracting the driver.

Friday

Make a group sports-safety mural showing a variety of sports (including dancing) and the appropriate clothing and equipment that should be worn. Talk about their sports experiences with injuries they or others have suffered and how those injuries might have been prevented.

The World of Books

Topic Summary

Explore the wonderful world of books and children's literature with your class this week and create READING excitement!

Words to Know

literature	novel
illustrator	illustration
non-fiction	fiction
character	plot
reference	encyclopedia
almanac	Thesaurus

Extra Reference:

READING IS FUNDAMENTAL
Smithsonian Institution, Suite 500, 600 Maryland Avenue, S.W.
Washington, DC 20560. *(Send for an activities packet on READING IS FUN week. Direct inquiries to the Director of Special Projects.)*

Community Resources

• **Ask** the local librarian to select some good books to share.

• **Garage sales** and **swap meets** for inexpensive ways to purchase books for the classroom

• **Invite** the owner of the local **book store** to bring samples to class.

• **Sponsor** a school visit by an author or illustrator of childrens' literature.

References

1. *The Newbery Award Winners: The Books and Their Authors The Caldecott Award: The Books and Their Authors*, Bertha Woolman, T.S. Denison & Co., (ready reference)
2. *Literary Prizes and Their Winners*, R.R. Bowker, NY, (ready reference)
3. *The New Read-Aloud Handbook*, Jim Trelease
4. *Choosing Books for Kids: How to Choose the Right Book for the Right Child at the Right Time*, Barbara Brenner and the Bank Street College of Education Staff.
5. *Leading to Reading,* Barbara Lee and Marsha K. Rudman

Additional Ideas

• **Start** a "Share a Book" program. Invite senior citizens, other classes and parents into your classroom to read with your students.
• **Visit** a local book store. Ask the owner to explain how the books are organized on the shelves.

The World of Books

Monday

Share a variety of picture books so children can study the art and illustrations. Discuss the variety of artwork and the kinds of art medium that were used. Talk about how a picture can tell a story. Read several of the books aloud.

Tuesday

Bring a sampling of *non-fiction* books to class. Point out that these books are based on *fact*. Together, make a list of *subjects* that an author of a non-fiction book might write about. Ask the class to choose a *biography* to read together in the future.

Wednesday

Explain the difference between a *fiction* and a *non-fiction* book. Discuss the different kinds of books available to children—adventure, mystery, sports, human nature, novels, short stories, poetry and so on. Take a poll to find out which kind each student prefers to read.

Thursday

Ask every student to bring their *favorite* book to school to share with classmates. Ask them to show the book and explain briefly why it appeals to them so much. Is it a book mom or dad has read often to them? Do they especially like the pictures? Was it an exciting *plot*? Is there a *character* they identified with or liked?

Friday

Explore the world of *reference* books. Show the children samples of *encyclopedias, Thesaurus, rhyming dictionaries, almanacs* and other factual books. Explain how to use each. Divide into groups and play a "searching for facts" game. Even younger students can be involved by indicating in which book they think they might find the requested information.

Health, Hygiene and Nutrition

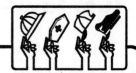

Topic Summary

Taking good care of your body is one of the most important things you can do for yourself. Introduce children to a daily program of proper diet, exercise and personal hygiene.

Words to Know

hygiene	nutrition
grooming	appearance
balanced diet	exercise
cleanliness	healthy
energy	nutrients
vitamins	posture
manicure	personal care
junk food	nutritious

Community Resources

- **Ask** your school district dietician and menu planner for information on diet and school lunches.
- **Invite** professionals in the field of body care–dermatologists, manicurists–to demonstrate cleanliness and care tips.
- **Visit** a fitness center to find out about the effects of exercise on the body.
- **Ask** a community dentist or hygienist to demonstrate good brushing and flossing methods.

References

1. *Keeping Clean*, Vicki Cobb, Lippincott
2. *Your Health* series, Dorothy Baldwin, Rourke Enterprises.
   Titles include:

Health and Food	*Health and Exercise*
Health and Drugs	*Health and Feelings*
Health and Friends	

3. *Magic Monsters Learn About Health*, Jane Belk Moncure, Children's Press
4. *Children Need Food*, Harry Undy, Cavendish

Additional Ideas

Research the nutritional and vitamin content of a variety of foods.
Establish an on-going physical fitness program.
Set up a center that where students can share newly-learned tips about health and hygiene.

Health, Hygiene and Nutrition

Monday

Begin the week with a discussion about an extremely important part of good health–the food we eat. Bring a variety of food to display. Ask students to help you sort the food into two categories– healthy, nutritious food and junk food. Explain which foods are rich in *vitamins* and *nutrients*. Talk about the dangers of too much sugar and fat in a diet. Ask them which foods they think provide the best *energy*. Plan several meals that create a *balanced diet*.

Tuesday

Explain that, along with eating nutritious food, *exercise* is important to maintaining a healthy body. Together, create a simple daily exercise program children can follow either at home or school. Practice each exercise then talk about how they can incorporate this program into their daily routines. Share stories about sports and dance programs in which students are currently participating.

Wednesday

Drinking several glasses of water a day helps keep the body cleansed and healthy. Provide a container filled with a day's recommended quota of drinking water and cup for each student. Ask them to drink all the water in the container by the end of the day. You can stop during the day to drink a cup together. This "hands-on" approach will familiarize students with the actual volume of liquid they should drink.

Thursday

Set up several "personal care" centers in the classroom to rotate through during the day. At each center provide the care products listed below and demonstrate their use.
Hand and nail–soap, small nail brush, nail trimmers, hand lotion
Hair–shampoo, conditioner, comb, brush
Mouth and teeth–toothbrush, dental floss, mouthwash
Stress the importance of keeping the skin, hair, mouth and body fresh and clean.

Friday

Emphasis is on *personal appearance*–good *posture* and *grooming*. To demonstrate the importance, take two students aside and dress one neatly and the other in sloppy, dirty clothes. Ask the student dressed neatly to stand with good body posture. Ask the second student to slouch. Then bring the students before their classmates. Ask the classmates to give their "impressions" of the two different appearances. Practice good posture together.

Music Appreciation

Topic Summary

Fill your classroom with "the sound of music". Expand students' musical horizons by introducing them to a variety of music, composers and instruments. Help them to see the world of music available beyond the popular music they listen to.

Words to Know

lyrics	melody
musician	instrument
composer	orchestra
band	concert
opera	waltz
folk music	instrumental
classical	popular
jazz	vocal
"jam" session	mood music
notes	chords
key	chant

Community Resources

- **Invite** a music teacher to demonstrate the steps in learning a musical instrument.
- **Explore** the tapes and records available for check out at the library.
- **Check** the schedules of local bands or orchestras for any concerts you might attend as a class.
- **Arrange** a field trip to a community college class or practice session.
- **Ask** music stores for samples or ideas to share.

References

1. *The Story of Music*, Brett and Ingman, Taplinger Publishing Co.
2. *Music, An Illustrated Encyclopedia*, Neil Ardley, Facts on File (reference)
3. *The Oxford First Companion to Music*, Kenneth Valerie McLeish, Oxford University Press (reference)
4. *Music*, Carole Green, Children's Press
5. *Great Composers*, Piero Ventura, G.P. Putnam's Sons

Additional Ideas

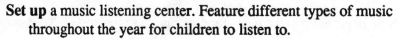
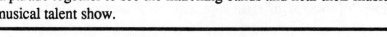

Set up a music listening center. Feature different types of music throughout the year for children to listen to.

Arrange to have the local high school band or orchestra perform for your school.

Attend a parade together to see the marching bands and hear their music.

Plan a musical talent show.

Music Appreciation

Monday

Spend the day playing a variety of background music while the children work. Include *opera*, soft *mood music, jazz, swing* etc. At the end of the day, ask children to evaluate the music. Which did they like? What effect did the different music have on them? Did one make them feel calmer than another? Which did they prefer to listen to? play to? work to? Why?

Tuesday

Obtain a variety of musical *instruments* from the school district, on loan from a local store or brought by students and their parents to have on display in the classroom. Demonstrate each one. (You don't have to be an accomplished musician to do this!) Discuss the variety of sounds the instruments make. Have an impromptu "jam session".

Wednesday

Introduce students to *composers*. Play samples of their works. Check out biographies for students to read. Choose one to read aloud. Bring in some sheet music to look at together. Talk about the elements on the page—notes, chords, keys.

Thursday

Explore *folk music* from around the world. Check the library for tapes or records with samples of folk music to listen to. Provide simple musical instruments—drums, tambourines, bells, auto-harp. Teach the children to chant (one group repeats what the other group says). Create some original classroom folk music!

Friday

Discuss the difference between *instrumental* music and music with *lyrics*. Listen to some "old and new standards" and discuss the lyrics. What do they mean? Are there lessons to be learned? Are they just for fun?

Art Appreciation

Topic Summary

Introduce your class to various types of art. Focus on the impressionist painters and their techniques and explore their rich world of color.

Words to Know

medium
oil paints
acrylic paints
watercolor paints
tempera paints
colored pencil
pastels
charcoal
palette
canvas

pure color
sculpture
sculptor
impressionism
pointilism
still life
landscape
seascape
portrait

Community Resources

- **Visit** local museums.

- **Find out** about art galleries that will provide lectures and walk-throughs

- **Check out** a picture file of the great artists from the local library

- **Invite** an artist from a local art association to demonstrate techniques in class.

References

1. *ABC-Museum of Fine Arts*, Florence Casson Mayers, Harry N. Abrams, Inc.
2. *Meet Edgar Degas*, Anne Newlands, J.B. Lippincott
3. *Charcoal and Pastel*, Don Bolognese and Elaine Raphael, Franklin Watts
4. *Alexander Calder and His Magical Mobiles*, Jean Lipman and Margaret Aspinwall, Hudson Hills Press, Inc.
5. *World Book Encyclopedia* (Look under "Paintings" for color reproductions of the impressionist painters.)

Additional Ideas

- **Turn** the school library or auditorium into an **Art Gallery** displaying student artwork. Invite classes and parents to visit the gallery.
- **Learn** about how pictures are framed and matted.

Art Appreciation

Monday

Experiment with various art mediums. If possible, have samples of paints available to explain the qualities of each type:

- **oil**—thick, rich colors, easy to work with and cover mistakes, long drying time (can be months). Used by the great masters.
- **acrylic**—similar in texture to oil paints but dries quickly.
- **watercolor**—translucent, soft quality. Hard to control. Dries quickly.
- **pastels**—a 'paste' of pigments and gum. Colors are bright and easy to work with although they create dust and can be messy.

Tuesday

Learn about impressionism! Using pictures from the local library picture files or from books of the impressionists, show children, up close, the technique of "pointilism." This was the technique developed by the French impressionists where they applied color in small individual spots or strokes of "pure" color instead of mixing it on the palette. The spots or strokes are applied to a surface so that from a distance they blend together to show an object. (The word "pointilism" is from *pointiller* meaning 'to stipple.')

Wednesday

Practice the impressionist's technique. Provide materials for children to use. Crayons, markers, pastels work well in addition to paints. If possible, take children outdoors for the practice session and have them work by copying something they are looking at: flowers, a table with some still life objects, etc. The impressionist painters always painted outdoors in natural light and only used pure colors.

Thursday

Introduce the French impressionist painters—Edouard Manet, Camille Pissarro, Edgar Degas, Claude Monet and Pierre Auguste Renoir. The post-impressionists included Paul Cezanne, Paul Gaugin, Vincent van Gogh, Georges Seurat and Henri de Toulouse-Latrec. Select 1 or 2 "easy" works and allow children to try to copy the work. Set up a gallery to display the copies.

Friday

Visit a museum to see the variety of types of art from paintings and sculpture to mobiles and weavings. If a museum is not available to visit, arrange for a walk-through at a local art gallery—or obtain books from the library.

Ecology Awareness

Topic Summary

Make students conscious of the environment and the need to work together to preserve our natural resources. Focus on our need to be aware of the various ecosystems and their interdependence on one another.

Words to Know

air pollution	oil spill
atmosphere	ozone layer
biodegradable	pesticide
conservation	plastics
disposable	recycle
drought	renewable
dump	smog
Earth Day	solar power
ecology	styrofoam
endangered species	throw-away society
environment	toxic
landfill	water pollution
natural	wilderness
non-toxic	wildlife

Community Resources

- **Visit a**
  - recycling center
  - landfill
  - bird sanctuary

- **Ask** a city council member to speak to you about steps the local government has taken toward improving our environment.

- **Find out** if there is a tree farm in your area and invite its owner to visit your class.

References

1. *Environment*, David Cook, Crown Publishers, Inc.

2. *The Environment*, Irving Adler, John Day Co.

3. *The Forest*, David Bellamy, Crown Publishers

4. *Ponds and Streams*, Judith Court, Franklin Watts

Additional Ideas

- **Set up** a classroom—or school-wide—recycling program.
- **Make** recycled paper
- **Make** a chart showing the time required for specific items of trash to decompose.

Ecology Awareness

Monday

Learn about landfills! What is a landfill? Where is the closest one to our community? What types of materials are dumped into the landfill? What can be done to make it a safe landfill? What can be done with trash instead of taking it to a landfill?

Divide answers to the last questions into two groups—those that eliminate a problem and those that cause another problem.

Tuesday

Bring an item from the family's trash for use in a group art project. Work cooperatively in groups of 4-5 creating artwork utilizing everyone's trash. Title each project. Have an exhibit to show finished works and call it "Group Garbage Art."

Wednesday

Discuss air pollution. What causes air pollution in our community? Why do you suppose some cities have major air pollution problems and other cities don't? As a cooperative class project, have children work on a large mural depicting the various sources of air pollution. Have children plan ahead so the mural shows a variety of causes.

Thursday

Have a "White Elephant Sale" as part of a campaign to "reduce, reuse, repair and recycle." Ask each student to bring in an article from home (with parents' permission) that the family no longer needs or wants. Set up an area for displaying the items. Decide if children will trade or give-away their donations.

Friday

Research these personalities who have actively worked to improve the environment:

John Muir	George Washington Carver	Denis Hayes
Robert Redford	John James Audubon	Johnny Appleseed
Theodore Roosevelt	Henry David Thoreau	

Read about these environmental activists to younger students.

Ask each group of 2-4 students to report their findings in one of the following ways: a skit, an oral report, an original poem or song, a chart.

In an Emergency

Topic Summary

It's important for everyone to know how to handle any emergency–big or small. From simple cuts to natural disasters, the threat of an emergency lives with us daily. This week introduce students to emergency and first aid basics.

Words to Know

emergency	medical emergency
First Aid	natural disaster
poison	Cardio-pulmonary
"drop and roll"	Resuscitation
evacuation	Heimlich maneuver
ambulance	paramedic
volunteer	American Red Cross
escape route	shelter
fire drill	

Community Resources

- **Ask** a volunteer from your local chapter of the American Red Cross to speak in your classroom
- **Visit** your community fire and police departments.
- **Find out** about disaster teams set up by your local government.
- **Invite** a nurse or doctor to demonstrate first aid.
- **Learn** about emergencies faced by ambulance drivers and paramedics.

References

1. *First Aid for Kids*, Barrows Educational Services
2. *Emergency Preparedness*, Boy Scouts of America
3. *Coping with Natural Disasters*, Carline Arnold, Walker & Co.
4. *Disaster!* –a series from Children' Press, includes earthquakes, floods, tornadoes, volcanoes, blizzards, droughts.
5. *The Survival Book*, Tegner and McGrath, Bantam Books

Additional Ideas

- **Practice** first aid treatments for a variety of emergencies
- **Learn** about your school's plan in the event of an emergency.
- **Research** careers that involve first aid and emergencies. Interview several people pursuing these careers.
- **Make** a list of organizations that provide disaster relief. Find out how to become a volunteer.

Theme Weeks
In an Emergency

Monday

Discuss emergencies children may have to face. Make a chart of all the *telephone numbers* they might need in an emergency. Include hospital emergency room, doctor, police and fire departments, ambulance service, poison control center and, of course, **911**. Discuss the appropriate times to use the different numbers. Practice making proper emergency calls, giving necessary information and following the directions given.

Tuesday

Assemble a *FIRST AID KIT* for the classroom. Discuss the uses for each item in the kit. Items to include in the kit are first aid book, scissors, distilled water (in unbreakable container), tweezers, sewing needle, matches, adhesive bandages, adhesive tape, sterile gauze, cotton swabs, bandaids, soap. Practicing some basic first aid skills can help prepare children in the event of a small medical emergency.

Wednesday

Invite a trained person to come to class and demonstrate *Cardiopulmonary Resuscitation* (CPR) and the *Heimlich Maneuver* (for choking). Stress the importance of knowing both techniques. Practice each in a simulated situation.

Thursday

Practice what to do in the event of fire. Teach students to stay low to the floor and to "drop and roll" should their clothing catch on fire. Ask them to plan two *escape routes* out of their homes and bring the map to school to share. Arrange to have a practice fire drill during the day at school.

Friday

Discuss *natural disasters*–floods, earthquakes, tornadoes, blizzards, hurricanes, cyclones, volcanoes and "tsunami" (tidal wave). Send home a list of general *Home Emergency Supplies*. Then talk about the particular supplies, preparation and procedures necessary for the potential natural emergencies in your particular area. (See *Information Inventory* for complete lists of supplies and procedures.)

CLASSROOM KICKOFF • © EDUPRESS

243

The Election Process

Topic Summary

In a democratic society, voters elect government leaders to make rules for the people. In the United States, Election Day is always held on the first Tuesday following the first Monday in November.

Words to Know

candidates
campaign
senator
representative
prime minister
parliament
democracy
dictatorship

poll
vote
ballot
city government
county government
state government
national government

Community Resources

- **Visit** political party headquarters

- **Invite** local politicians to speak at school

- **Listen** to a candidate speak on a local campaign stop

- **Attend** a city council meeting

References

1. *Voting and Elections*, Dennis B. Fradin
   Childrens Press
2. *The Story of Presidential Elections*, Jim Hargrove
   Childrens Press
3. *How Elections Work in America*, Jules Archer
   Winners and Losers
4. *Women Win the Vote*, Betsy Covington Smith
   Silver Burdett Press, Inc.

Additional Ideas

Design a sample ballot.

Make a polling booth out of a refrigerator box.

The Election Process

Monday

Set up a balloting system in your classroom the week prior to Election Day, so that students may pretend to vote for actual candidates. Allow the class to decide the candidates they will vote for—on a local, city, state or national level. Prepare mock secret ballots that children will cast. You may want to have your elections on Election Day so students 'feel the mood'. Following actual elections, compare class elections with the real results. Did your class' choices win "by a landslide" or "by a narrow margin?"

Tuesday

Write sayings or slogans that reflect a candidate's issues. Provide samples for starters. A simple but popular one was **I LIKE IKE** which did not reflect an issue but was very persuasive in getting votes. Decide on 1 or 2 'best' slogans and have children create campaign buttons to wear.

Wednesday

Create campaign posters. If possible, bring in some actual campaign posters as samples. Have students design posters and/or handouts for a candidate of their choice.

Thursday

Discuss the difference between a democracy and a dictatorship. What freedoms are absent in a dictatorship? What class or school activities show the democratic method? (voting for student council, PTA officers, etc.) What class or school activities resemble a dictatorship? (the days and hours you must attend school, completing assignments or being penalized, etc.)

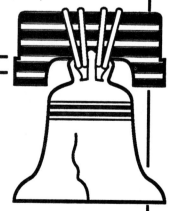

Friday

View filmstrips on past presidents. Try to locate video tapes or records of speeches of past presidents for children to listen to. What makes some speeches outstanding while others are boring?

Drug Awareness

Topic Summary

One of the most important lessons a child will learn is to say "NO" to drugs. Statistics show that pressure to try alcohol and other drugs is felt even in the elementary grades. This week, increase student knowledge of the types and dangers of drugs. Provide them with the social tools necessary for saying "NO".

Words to Know

alcohol	marijuana
heroin	cocaine & crack
tobacco	inhalants
amphetamines	peer pressure
habit-forming	dependence
deadly	addictive

NOTE: Before you begin a drug awareness program in your classroom check with your principal for school district guidelines and curriculum.

Community Resources

- **Visit** a drug rehabilitation center.

- **Invite** the director of a drug prevention program to speak in your class.

- **Ask** high school students to share the stories of their battle with drugs.

- **Find** out about drug and alcohol treatment centers.

References

1. *Understanding Drugs*–an in-depth information series covering all aspects of drugs. Titles include Marijuana, Alcohol, Heroin, Cocaine and Crack, Tobacco and Inhalants.
2. *You Can Say No To a Drink or a Drug*, Susan Newman, Perigee Books
3. *It's O.K.To Say No To Drugs*, Alan Garner

Additional Ideas

Create an "It's O.K. to Share" program in your school. Let children know that they can tell any adult that they have been confronted with drug use. Assure them that all information is confidential.
Conduct Parent Education days. Invite parents to class to have open discussions with children.

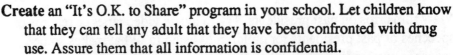

Drug Awareness

Monday

Discuss various kinds of drugs. Ask students which ones they know about. Talk about the addictive nature and dangers of drugs. Introduce the week by reading several books about drugs throughout the day. Find out about the different, long-term effects of taking drugs. Ask students to be looking and listening for advertisements on television, radio and magazines that relate an anti-drug message. Encourage them to bring the ads to class on Friday.

Tuesday

Make a chart. Divide it into two sections. On one half list the **PROS** of taking drugs. On the other half, list the **CONS** of taking drugs. Talk about the results of the chart.

Wednesday

Role play different peer-group situations students may encounter that would involve taking of drugs. Even younger children can relate to being at a party and being offered something they don't want or can't have. Role play what to do if they know someone who is involved with taking drugs.

Thursday

Design anti-drug posters. Make up several slogans to use. Display the posters around school–in the library, the office, the principal's office, hallways, other classrooms.

Friday

Share the advertisements that students saw or found relating an anti-drug message. *(See Monday.)* What did they learn from the ads? Which advertisement affected them the most? As a group or on their own, ask children to write and design an effective anti-drug advertisement.

Instant Activity

Class Name Search

Teacher directions:
Create a name search using the first names of students in your class. (See pages 10-11.) Make a copy for each child.

Student directions:
Use your class list to find classmate names. Look for first names only. Remember, the names can be forward, up, down, diagonal or backward!

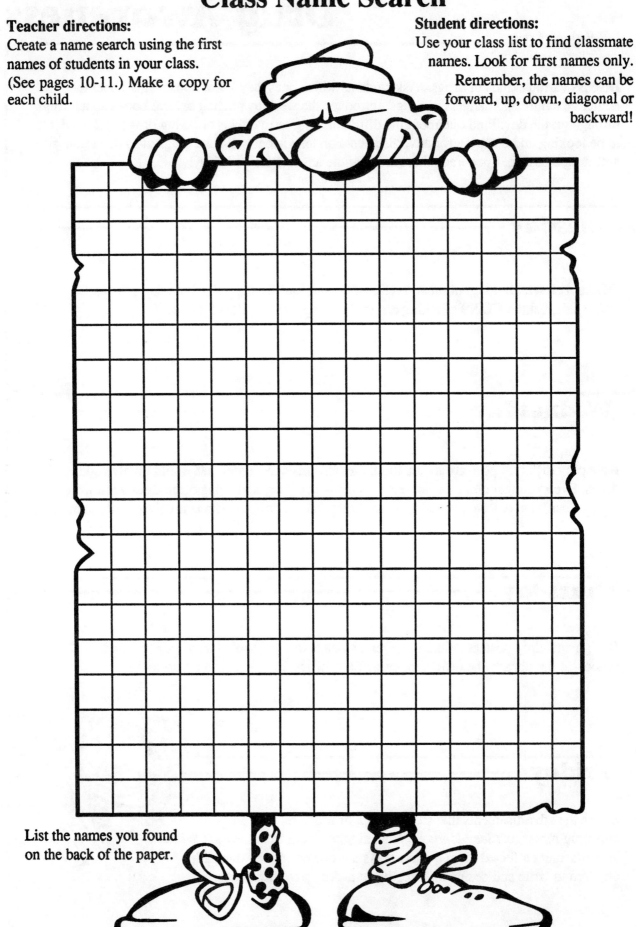

List the names you found on the back of the paper.

Fun with Names

> *Use your class list to answer these name questions.*

Write the last name(s) with the most letters: Write the first name(s) with the fewest letters:

_____

_____

Is there a name that more than one student has? Write the name(s) below:

Count the letters in each of the last names. Keep track below. Fill in the horizontal bar graph to show the results.

3															
4															
5															
6															
7															
8															
9 or more															

Count the names that end in these letters.
Write the total next to the letter.

    First Names   Last Names

Y

M

T

Are there any hyphenated names?
Write them here:

Are there any names pronounced the same but spelled differently?
Write them here: _____

Which name do you think is the most unusual? _____

Which name is the easiest to remember? _____

How Many?

Take a look around your classroom and count how many . . .

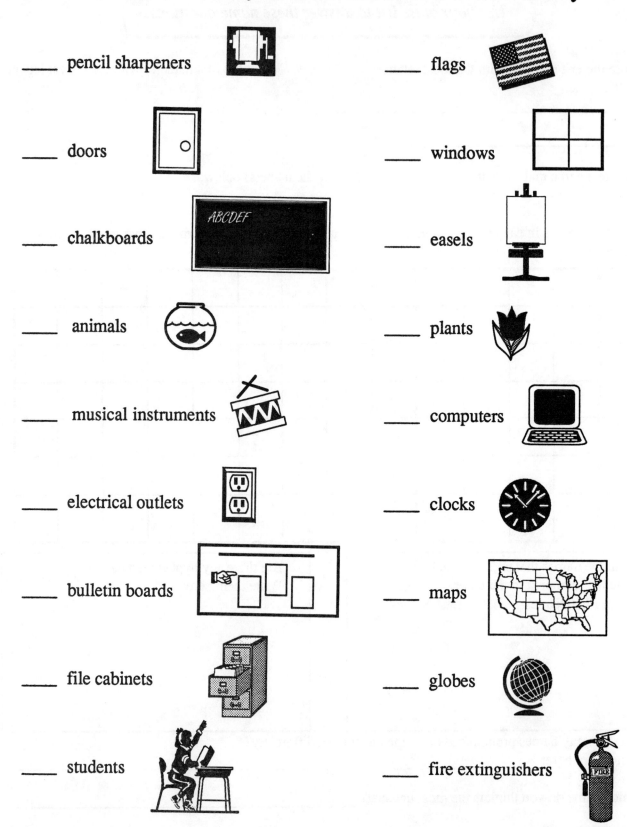

____ pencil sharpeners

____ doors

____ chalkboards

____ animals

____ musical instruments

____ electrical outlets

____ bulletin boards

____ file cabinets

____ students

____ flags

____ windows

____ easels

____ plants

____ computers

____ clocks

____ maps

____ globes

____ fire extinguishers

PERSONAL PUZZLE

Use crayons to personalize this puzzle. Paste it to sturdy construction paper, cut it out, put your initials on the back of each piece and store it in an envelope. Trade your puzzle with a classmate and put them back together during your free time.

Circle Solutions

> *Here are two kinds of solutions that will get you going in circles!*
> *Look at the samples, then try two on your own, turn your paper*
> *over and make two more!*

Word Circles

Around the outside of a circle, print a word. Look at the last letter. Think of another word that begins with that letter and write it down next to the first word. Continue around the circle. The last word you print must end with the first letter of the first word you wrote! You cannot use the same word twice

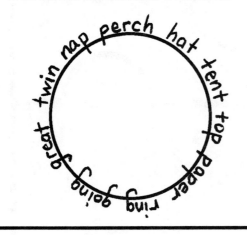

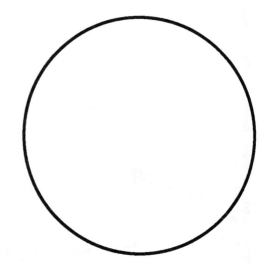

Math Circles

Write a simple math problem on the circle. The next problem must begin with the answer to the previous one. Continue around the circle. The solution to the last problem must equal the number you started with.

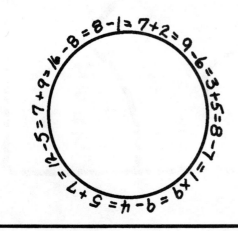

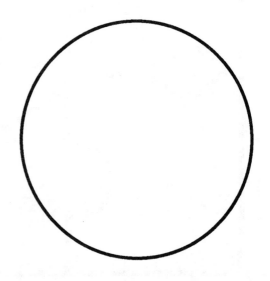

Fun with Boxes

Fill each box with a different picture. Put a check mark in front of the category you have chosen (or the one your teacher has assigned). Then put on your thinking cap and go to work!

- ❑ fruits and vegetables
- ❑ sporting equipment
- ❑ holiday symbols
- ❑ things you like

- ❑ designs and patterns
- ❑ words that start with the same letter
- ❑ things that remind you of school
- ❑ other _____

Just Imagine!

Use your imagination. List two things you think each picture could be.
Try the first one with your classmates;
then you're on your own.

What could this be?

_____

_____

What's in the pumpkin?

_____

_____

What's in this egg?

_____

_____

What could this be?

_____

_____

What did he eat?

_____

_____

What's underground?

_____

_____

Pick one of your answers and write or tell more about it.

Designer Squares

Count, follow directions, create—no matter how often you do this activity, each time will turn out different! The design will be your personal creation. However, you must include these squares:

5 polka dot		3 stripes		4 wavy lines	
7 red		6 blue		4 orange	
2 green		5 purple		6 yellow	

When you're done, compare your creation with your classmates'. Are any two the same?

This activity can be done as a class, in a small group or individually.

Other Ways to Say It

It's important to have the tools to make writing more colorful. This activity will help you learn about one of the important tools—word choices. In the available space, write as many other ways as you can think of to say the word in bold letters. If you can't spell the word, sound it out.

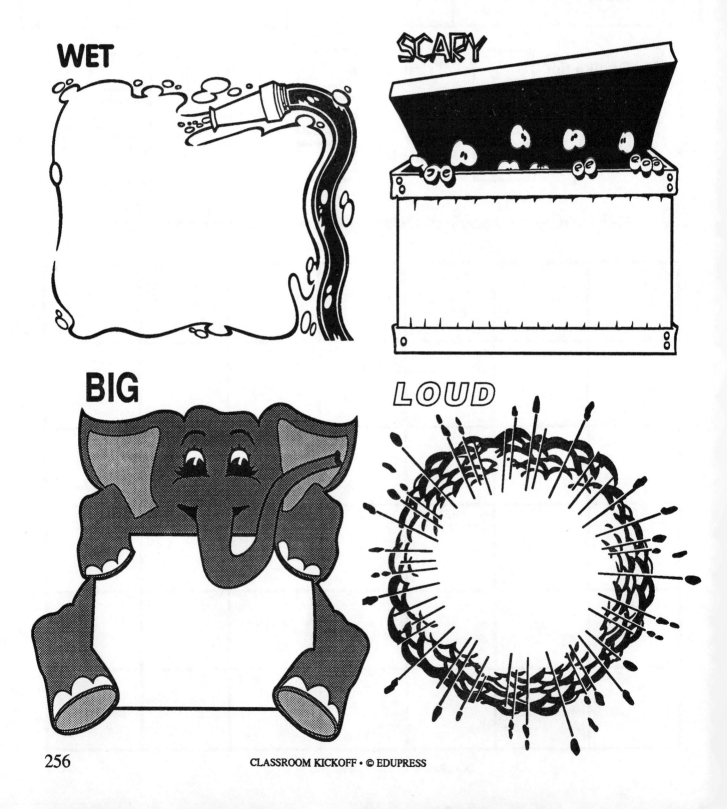

WET

SCARY

BIG

LOUD

CLASSROOM KICKOFF • © EDUPRESS

Name Calling!

We have names for just about everything! Pretend that your job is "Official Namer." You are responsible for creating original and imaginative names for all kinds of things. Write your "creations" in the space provided.

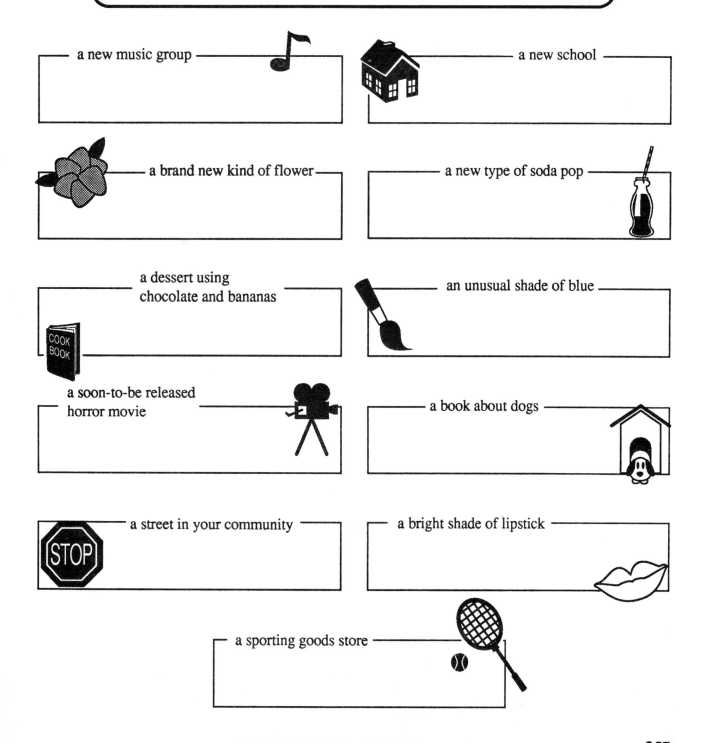

a new music group

a new school

a brand new kind of flower

a new type of soda pop

a dessert using chocolate and bananas

an unusual shade of blue

a soon-to-be released horror movie

a book about dogs

a street in your community

a bright shade of lipstick

a sporting goods store

Instant Activity

Going in Circles

As you look around you will find circles everywhere! Look at what was created with these circles.

Now create some circle pictures of your own. Look in picture books and magazines for ideas.

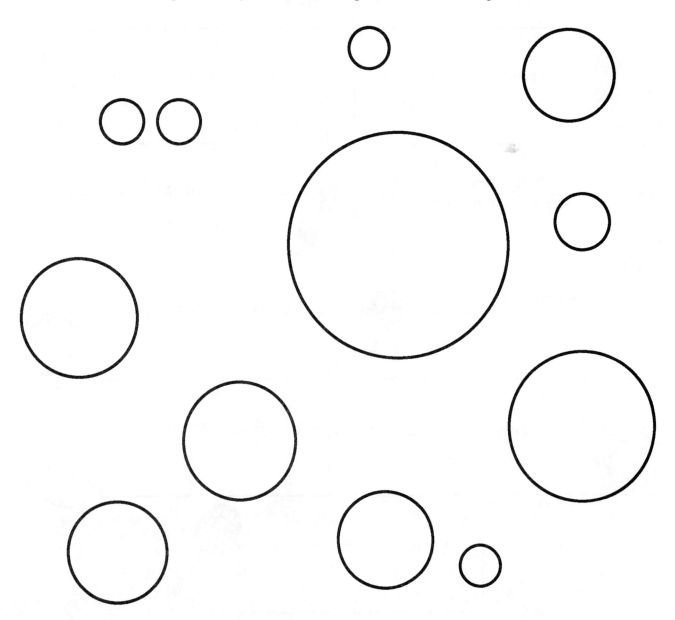

A Letter From...

It takes many people working together to make your school a special place for all its students. Think about some of the jobs people have at your school. Try to imagine yourself in that job. What kinds of things could students do to help you? What kind of behavior would you expect from them?

Tell **your** students in a short letter. If you would like to do more letters than the three below, choose someone else who works at your school and write a letter from one of them.

Dear Students,

_____

_____

_____

_____

_____

From,
Your Principal

Dear Students,

_____

_____

_____

_____

_____

From,
Your Librarian

Dear Students

_____

_____

_____

_____

_____

From,
Your Custodian

SEPTEMBER
Around the World
...Holidays and Happenings

*Summer ends and autumn begins ... harvest time ... 30 days ... warm days, cool nights
Flower ... morning glory*

Changing dates:

Labor Day –*U.S., Canada*–first Monday

Native American Day – *U.S.*–fourth Friday

Other Dates:

4   **Sunrise Dance**–*U.S.*–"sun" celebration;
White Mountain Apache Indians, Arizona

8   **International Literacy Day**–*worldwide*

14   **Monarch Butterfly Migration**–*U.S., Canada*–
hundreds of thousands of butterflies migrate south,
always landing in the same areas

16   **Mid-autumn Festival**–*China*–harvest celebration;
the birthday of the moon

17   **Citizenship Day**–*U.S.*–celebrates the signing of the Constitution

19   **Yam Festival**–*Ghana*–celebration of the year's crop

21, 23 Autumn begins

25   **Yam Festival**–*Ghana*–celebration of the year's crop

26   **Johnny Appleseed** birthday, born 1774–*U.S.*

OCTOBER
Around the World
...Holidays and Happenings

Indian summer ... early signs of frost ... 31 days ... costumes and treats
Flower ... calendula

Changing dates:

Child Health Day–*U.S., Canada*–first Monday

Thanksgiving Day–*Canada*–second Monday

World Series–*Canada, U.S.*–baseball championships

Other dates:

5   **Nairobi Show**–*Kenya*–annual agricultural fair featuring fruits and vegetables

9   **Fire Prevention Day**–*U.S.*
      Hangul Nal–*Korea*–children have no classes but go to school for calligraphy contests

11   **Simhat Torah**–*Jewish*–lettered scrolls of the Torah are read

12   **ColumbusDay**–*U.S., Canada*–celebrates arrival in America on Oct. 12, 1492)

14   **White Sunday**–*Western Samoa*–roles reversed.
      Parents cook **instead** of children who begin cooking for the family at age 10!

15   **Poetry Day**–*U.S., Canada*

16   **World Food Day**–*worldwide*

22   **Rainmaking Cermony**–*South Africa*

24   **United Nations Day**–*worldwide*
      celebrates the beginning of the organization in 1945

31   **Halloween**–*U.S., Canada, Great Britain, Ireland*

NOVEMBER
Around the World
...Holidays and Happenings

Trees are bare ... time to give thanks ... 30 days ... nature at rest
Flower ... morning glory

Changing dates:

Thanksgiving–*U.S.*–fourth Thursday

Election Day–*U.S.*–the first Tuesday after the first Monday

Children's Book Week

Other dates:

1   **Divali**–*Hindu*–homes are cleaned, floors decorated with powdered paint

9   **Wax Festival**–*Morocco*–candlemakers carve shapes out of colored wax

10   **Rebenlichter**–*Switzerland*–
children hollow out white turnips and carve patterns in the surface

11   **Veterans' Day, ArmisticeDay**– *U.S., Canada, England, France*
honors those who served in armed forces

15   **Shichi-Go-San**–*Japan*–celebrates all Japanese children who are seven, five
and three years old. Children collect treats in paper bags printed
with good luck signs.

18   **Birthday of Mickey Mouse**–*worldwide*

19   **Discovery Day**–*Puerto Rico*

21   **Anniversary of man's first flight in a balloon**–*France*

DECEMBER
Around the World
...Holidays and Happenings

Birds fly to warmer climates ... nature prepares for winter ... 31 days ... gift giving
Flower ... holly , narcissus, poinsettia

Changing dates:

Hanukkah–*Jewish*–lasts for eight days beginning on the twenty-fifth day
of the lunar month of Kislev (November-December)

Other dates:

6   **St. NicholasDay**–*Europe*–St. Nicholas brings gifts to children

11   **Birthday of UNICEF**–*worldwide*–honors the establishment of the
United Nations Children's Emergency Fund

13   **Luciadagen**–*Sweden*–oldest child in family wears white robe, red sash
and a crown of lighted candles honoring Lucia, the Queen of Light

15   **Bill of Rights Day**–*U.S.*–celebrates the adoption of the Bill of Rights in1789

17   **Wright Brothers Day**–*U.S.*–celebrates the first airplane flight

21   **Forefathers' Day**–*New England*–commemorates the landing
of the Pilgrims at the site where they settled

21,22 Winter begins

25   **Christmas**

JANUARY
Around the World
...Holidays and Happenings

Animals hibernate ... snowflakes and snowmen ... 31 days ... jackets and mittens
Flower ... carnation, snowdrop

Changing dates:

Other dates:

1   **New Year's Day**–*worldwide*–the beginning of the new year

2   **Kakizome**–*Japan*–First writing of the year; usually a poem or proverb

10 **Iroquois midwinter Ceremony**–*U.S., Canada*–false face masks are made and worn

14 **Pongol**–*India*–harvest festival honoring the sun and rain that ripen rice crops

15 **Martin Luther King Day**–*U.S.*–Martin Luther King born 1929

17 **San Antonio Abad**–*Mexico*–honoring patron saint of animals;
        dress up animals for a parade

19 **Kite Festival**–*Singapore*–homemade kite-flying contest

20 **Inauguration Day**–*U.S.*

27 **Lewis Carroll birthday**–*worldwide*–author of *Alice's Adventures in Wonderland*

28 **Tu Bishvat**–*Jewish*–tree planted for each baby born in the year

31 **Soldag**–*Norway*–celebrates the reappearance of the sun

FEBRUARY
Around the World
...Holidays and Happenings

Hearts and flowers ... Cupid's arrow ... 28 days ... leap year
Flower ... primrose

Changing dates:

President's Day–*U.S.*–third Monday, combined celebration honoring birthdates of George Washington and Abraham Lincoln

Other dates:

1   **National Freedom Day**–*U.S.*–marks the anniversary of an amendment to the Constitution to abolish slavery, 1865

2   **Groung-Hog Day (Candlemas)**–*worldwide*

6   **Sapporo Snow Festival**–*Japan*–snow sculpting

12   **Abraham Lincoln birthday,** 1809–*U.S.*

13   **Chinese New Year**–*China*

14   **Valentine's Da**y–*Canada, U.S., Europe*

19   **Kiddie Carnival**–*Trinidad & Tobago*–theme carnival for children

20   **Battles of the Flowers**–*France*–12 day festivities honoring flowers

22   **George Washington birthday,** *1732–U.S.*

25   **Mardi Gras Carnival**–*worldwide*

26   **Lantern Festival**–*China*

29   **Leap Year Day**–*worldwide*–once every four years

MARCH
Around the World
...Holidays and Happenings

Winter ends and spring begins ... shamrocks ... 31 days ... robins appear
Flower ... violet

Changing dates:

Purim—*Jewish*

Other dates:

1   **Whuppity Scoorie**—*Scotland*—*a celebration of the bells*

2   **Birthday of Dr. Seuss**—*U.S., Canada*—famous author of children's books

3   **Hina Matsuri**—*Japan*—Doll Festival

17   **St. Patrick's Day**—*U.S., Canada, Ireland*

21   **Noruz**—*Iran*—new year celebration

20,21 **Spring begins**

26   **Kuhio Day**—*U.S. (Hawaii)*—Prince Kuhio festival includes outrigger canoe races and hula dances

28   **Teacher's Day**—*Czechoslovakia*—children bring flowers and gifts to their teachers.

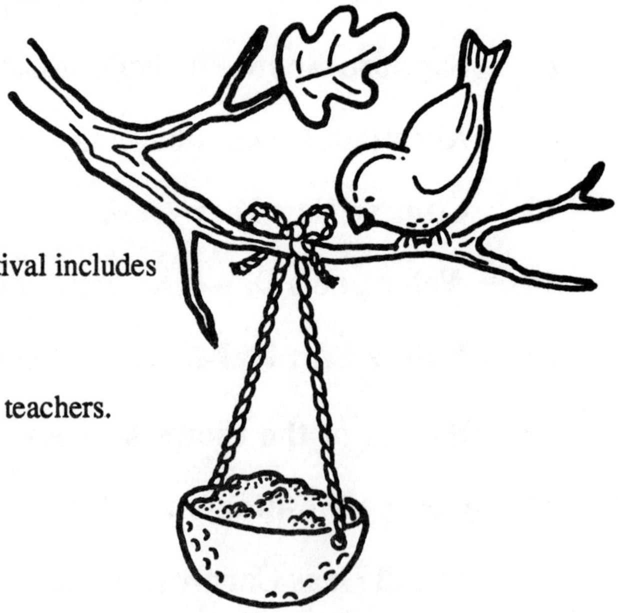

APRIL
Around the World
...Holidays and Happenings

Bunnies and baskets ... rain showers ... 30 days ... baseball begins
flower ... sweet pea, daisy

Changing dates:

Arbor Day–*U.S., Canada*–check your community calendar

Bird Day–*U.S.*–sometime during the second week; started by the Audubon Society

Easter–date determined by the moon; first Sunday after the first full moon after the 21st of March

Passover–*Jewish*

Patriot's Day–*U.S.*–third Monday;celebrated with reenactment of Paul Revere's ride

Other dates:

1 **April Fools' Day**–*U.S., Canada, Europe*–a time for practical jokes

2 **International Children's Book Day**–*worldwide*
   Date selected to honor Hans Christian Andersen's birthday.

6 **Qing Ming**–**China**–*Bright and Happy* celebration

7 **World Health Day**–worldwide

14 **Pan American Day**–*U.S., Mexico, Central and South America* friendship celebration

29 **Emperor's Birthday** –*Japan*

22 **Earth Day**–*U.S.*

23 **Children's Day**–*Turkey*–children take over the government
    and are awarded free privileges around their communities
    St George's Day–*England*–celebrates the popular legend that a brave knight named
    George slew a dragon to save the king's daughter

MAY
Around the World
... Holidays and Happenings

Outdoor festivals ... Maypoles ... 31 days ... flowers in full bloom
Flower ... lily of the valley

Changing dates:

Memorial (Decoration) Day–last Monday

Mother's Day–second Sunday

Armed Forces Day–third Saturday

Victoria (Queen's) Day–*Canada*–Monday before May 25

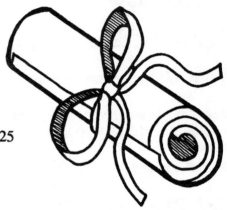

Other dates:

1   **May Day**–*worldwide*–flower festival, dancing around the May pole

3   **Constitution Day–** *Japan*

5   **Cinco de Mayo**–*Mexico*

12   **Cat Festival**–*Belgium*

15   **Leonardo da Vinci birthday**, 1452–*worldwide*–Italian painter, sculptor

22   **International Jumping Frog Jubilee**–*U.S*–the frog who covers
the greatest distance in three jumps wins the contest

25   **Bun Festival**–*Hong Kong*–children dress as figures of Chinese
history and appear in a parade

30   **Memorial Day**–*U.S.*–tradition of honoring U.S. soldiers

JUNE
Around the World
...Holidays and Happenings

Spring ends and summer begins ...flowers bloom ...30 days ...Bees are busy
Flower ...rose

Changing dates:

Father's Day–*U.S., Canada*–third Sunday

Other dates:

3   **Jefferson Davis birthday, 1808**–*U.S.*–southern states' celebration

5   **World Environment Day**–*worldwide*

6   **Top Spinning Contest**–*Malaysia*

10   **Maurice Sendak's birthday, 1928**–*U.S., Canada*–famous author
  and illustrator of children's books

14   **Flag Day**–*U.S.*

16   **Tano**–*Korea*–spring festival; boys have wrestling competition,
  girls have swinging contests

17   **Lily Festival**–*Japan*

21,22 Summer begins

JULY
Around the World
...Holidays and Happenings

Heatwaves ... fireworks ... 31 days ... starry nights and campouts
Flower ... water lily

Changing dates:

Cheyenne Frontier Days–*U.S.*–the people of Cheyenne, Wyoming,
    sponsor the world's largest outdoor rodeo

Tour de France–*France*–famous bicycle race

Other dates:

1   **Dominion Day**–Canada– also called Dominion Day;
        provinces united under one government, 1867

4   **Independence Day**–*U.S.*–birthday of the United States

7   **Fiesta de San Fermin**–*Spain*–running of the bulls in Pamplona

11   **E.B. White birthday**–*U.S., Canada*–author of children's novel, *Charlotte's Web*

14   **Bastille Day**–*France*–national holiday celebrating the
        beginning of the French Revolution

9   **Lobster Carnival**–*Canada*–the town of Pictou, Nova Scotia, celebrates the
        end of the fishing season with dancing and a parade

20   **Moon Day**–*worldwide*–celebrates the first landing of man on the moon, 1969

Emergency Preparation

*Although each disaster creates its own special problems, all share some common elements. The following list of emergency supplies to be kept at home is recommended by the **American Red Cross**. These enable a family to live independently for 72 hours or more after a major disaster. A two-week supply is recommended as a minimum reserve of water, food, medicine and other consumable items.*

Home Emergency Supplies

First Aid Kit	First Aid Book	water (2 qts/day per person)
food–canned or packaged	can opener	blankets
portable radio	batteries	fire extinguisher
flashlight	watch/clock	plastic trash bags
trash cans	soap/detergent	personal hygiene items
toilet paper	heavy shoes/gloves	candles
matches	knife	garden hose
barbecue/charcoal	sealable plastic bags	cooking/eating utensils
axe/shovel/broom	crescent wrench/pliers	screwdriver/hammer

In addition to being generally prepared for emergencies, there are particular things to remember for each kind of natural disaster.

Hurricanes/Floods:

If water is threatening, move everything possible to upper floors of the house. Try to disconnect electrical appliances. Turn off the main electrical switch and cover electrical outlets. Take important papers and prescription medicines or glasses. Do not drink faucet water until it is determined safe.

Earthquakes:

Do not store heavy objects on high shelves. Know how to turn off gas, electricity and water at the main valves. If indoors during an earthquake, get under a sturdy table, brace yourself in a doorway or corner or move to an inside hallway, if possible. Stay clear of windows, bookcases, heavy mirrors and china cabinets or other heavy furniture. If in a car, pull to the side of the road and stop. If outdoors, stay clear of buildings and bridges. If you are at home, turn off all utilities.

Blizzard:

Dress with several layers of protective clothing. Mittens are better than gloves. Hoods or scarves can be used to cover the mouth and protect the lungs from extremely cold air. Keep an emergency kit in the car–wool blankets, flares, flashlight, high energy foods. Avoid getting wet and cold. Most importantly, try not to go outdoors during a blizzard!

Tornadoes:

The safest place to be is in the basement of a building or in a "storm cellar". If those places are not nearby, get under a sturdy table or other heavy piece of furniture that protects from glass and other flying debris. If outside, lie down in a ditch or a deep hollow.

Field Trip Suggestions

Use these trip suggestions to highlight a unit, add an out-of-classroom activity to daily learning and show students how your local community works.

Exhibits and Lectures

Children's Museum
Art Museum
Natural History Museum
Planetarium
Local Historical Site
Local Craft Exhibits

Community Services

Car Wash
Lumber Yard
Water Department
Police Station
Fire Station
Post Office
Local Library
Bank

Telephone Company
Recycling Center
TV/Radio Station
Newspaper Plant
Nursing Home
Another School
Factory
Hotel/Motel

Transportation

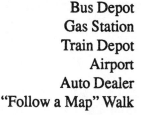

Bus Depot
Gas Station
Train Depot
Airport
Auto Dealer
"Follow a Map" Walk

Retail Stores

Florist
Beauty Salon
Fast Food Restaurant
Ethnic Restaurant
Doughnut Shop/Bakery
Ice Cream Shop
Supermarket
Pharmacy
Shoe Store
Parent-owned Store

Plants, Animals and Nature

Animal Shelter
Nursery
Zoo
Farmer's Market/Vegetable Farm
Picking-Fruit Farm
Horse Ranch
Lake/Sea/Beach
Forest/Wood
Botanical Gardens
Nature Walk
Veterinarian
Pet Store

Inventors and Inventions

Whether you've assigned a research paper or are looking for a discussion topic, this list of inventors and inventions should come in handy!

Inventor	Date	Invention
Prehistoric Man	2,600,000-8000 B.C.	bow, arrow, spear
Prehistoric Man	3000 B.C	wheel
Sumerians	3000 B.C.	writing
Ts'ai Lun	105	paper
Johannes Gutenberg	1455	printing "press"
Hand Lippershey	1608	telescope
George Stephenson	1825	locomotive
Charles Babbage	1833	computer
Louis Braille	1834	books for the blind
Walter Hunt	1849	safety pin
James Clerk Maxwell	1860	radar
Thomas Alva Edison	1880	phonograph, light bulb
Gottlieb Daimler, Karl Benz	1885	gasoline car
Whitcomb L. Judson	1893	zipper
Alexander Graham Bell	1895	telephone
Guglielmo Marconi	1895	radio
Marie Curie	1898	radiotherapy
Wilbur and Orville Wright	1903	airplane
John Logie Baird	1925	television
Clarence Birdseye	1925	frozen foods
Alexander Fleming	1928	penicillin

Looking for a Good Book?

Parents often ask teachers to recommend good books for their children. Here are some references that will help you compile a book list appropriate for your students. You may want to provide parents with this list, too, so that they may look for good books on their own. Check your public library for these titles. Encourage your school to add several to their teachers' reference library.

Subject Guide to Children's Books in Print
52,000 juvenile books by subject
R.R. Bowker
245 W.17th Street
New York, NY 10011

Stories to Tell & Read Aloud
Recommends Folk and Fairy tales
N.Y. Public Library/Office of Branch Libraries
455 Fifth Avenue
New York, NY 10016

Bulletin of Center for Children's Books
Evaluates juvenile books
University of Chicago Press
5720 S. Woodlawn Ave.
Chicago, IL 60637

Children's Authors and Illustrators
Biographical info./authors, illustrators
Gale Research Inc.
835 Penobscot Bldg.
Detroit, MI 48226-4094

Reading is Fundamental (RIF) Newsletter
Describes nationwide reading programs (U.S.)
Smithsonian Institute
900 Jefferson Drive
Washington, D.C. 20560

Book Mark
Reviews books, suggests activities
Children's literature in Review
Oakland University
Rochester, MI 48063

Int'l Directory/Children's Lit.
Covers organizations and book clubs
George Kurian Reference Books
PO Box 519 Baldwin Place
New York, NY 10505

Children's Book Review Serv.
Reviews books preschool-senior high
220 Berkeley Place —1-D
Brooklyn, NY 11217

Children's Literature Review
Critiques children's books
Gale Research Inc.
835 Penobscot Bldg.
Detroit, MI 48226-4094

Children's Book News
Reviews Canadian Books
Children's Book Centre
229 College St. W. 5th Floor
Toronto, Ontario M5T 1R4 Canada

Looking for Magazines?

Standard Periodical Directory
Listing and review by subject
Check: Educ., Children, Poetry/Creative writing

Guide to Periodicals/US, Canada
Listing and review by subject
Check: Educ., Children,Poetry/writing

Write to an Author

Use this list of publishers and their addresses if you or your students wish to contact an author or illustrator.

Generally, publishers will forward letters to their authors and artists for personal responses.

ATHENEUM CHILDREN'S BOOKS
866 Third Avenue
New York, NY 10022

AVON BOOKS
105 Madison Avenue
New York, NY 10016

BALLANTINE/DEL REY/FAWCETT BOOKS
RANDOM HOUSE
201 East 50th Street
New York, NY 10022

BANTAM BOOKS/BOOKS FOR YOUNG READERS
666 Fifth Avenue
New York, NY 10023

CAEDMON
1995 Broadway
New York, NY 10023

CAROLRHODA BOOKS
241 First Avenue North
Minneapolis, MN 55401

CLARION BOOKS/ HOUGHTON MIFFLIN
52 Vanderbilt Avenue
New York, NY 10017

T.Y. CROWELL JUNIOR BOOKS
HARPER & ROW JUNIOR BOOKS
10 East 53rd Street
New York, NY 10022

CROWN PUBLISHERS, INC.
225 Park Avenue South
New York, NY 10003

DELACORTE PRESS
BANTAM/DOUBLEDAY/DELL PUBLISHING GROUP
666 Fifth Avenue
New York, NY 10103

FARRAR, STRAUS & GIROUX
19 Union Square West
New York, NY 10003

E.P. DUTTON
2 Park Avenue
New York, NY 10016

GOLDEN BOOKS
850 Third Avenue
New York, NY 10022

GREENWILLOW BOOKS/ WILLIAM MORROW & CO.
105 Madison Avenue
New York, NY 10016

GROSSET & DUNLAP
200 Madison Avenue
New York, NY 10016

HARCOURT BRACE JAVONOVICH
1250 Sixth Avenue
San Diego, CA 92101

HOUGHTON MIFFLIN CO.
2 Park Street
Boston, MA 02108

ALFRED A. KNOPF, INC.
201 East 50th Street
New York, NY 10022

LITTLE, BROWN & CO., INC.
34 Beacon Street
Boston, MA 02108

LOTHROP, LEE & SHEPARD BOOKS
WILLIAM MORROW & CO.
105 Madison Avenue
New York, NY 10016

FRANKIN WATTS
387 Park Avenue South
New York, NY 10016

PUFFIN BOOKS
40 West 23rd Street
New York, NY 10010

SCHOLASTIC
730 Broadway
New York, NY 10003

CHARLES SCRIBNER'S SONS
MACMILLAN CHILDREN'S BOOK GROUP
866 Third Avenue
New York, NY 10022

VIKING PENGUIN CHILDREN'S BOOKS
40 West 23rd Street
New York, NY 10010

ALBERT WHITMAN & CO.
5747 West Howard Street
Niles, IL 60648

YEARLING BOOKS
DELL PUBLISHING
1 Dag Hammarskjold Plaza
New York, NY 10017

If you wish to contact a publisher not listed, look in "Writer's Marketplace" for address information. This is available at the public library.

Caldecott Medal Winners

The *Caldecott Medal*, named in honor of nineteenth-century English illustrator Randolph Caldecott, is awarded annually by the Association for Library Services to Children, a division of the American Library Association, to the *artist* of the most distinguished American picture book for children. The award began in 1938.

1991—Black and White
David Macauley

1990—Lon Po Po
Ed Young

1989—Song and Dance Man
Karen Ackerman
Illustrated by Stephen Gammell

1988—Owl Moon
Jane Yolen
Illustrated by John Schoenherr (Philomel)

1987—Hey, Al
Arthur Yorinks
Illustrated by Richard Egielski (Farrar)

1986—The Polar Express
Chris Van Allsburg (Houghton)

1985—Saint George and the Dragon
Retold by Margaret Hodges
Illustrated by Trina Schart Hyman
(Little, Brown)

1984—The Glorious Flight: Across the Channel with Louis Blériot
Alice and Martin Provensen (Viking)

1983—Shadow
Blaise Cendrars
Translated and illustrated by Marcia Brown
(Scribner)

1982—Jumanji
Chris Van Allsburg (Houghton)

1981—Fables
Arnold Lobel (Harper)

1980—Ox-Cart Man
Donald Hall
Pictures by Barbara Cooney (Viking)

1979—The Girl Who Loved Wild Horses
Paul Goble (Bradbury)

1978—Noah's Ark
Peter Spier (Doubleday)

1977—Ashanti to Zulu
Margaret Musgrove
Pictures by Leo and Diane Dillon (Dial)

1976—Why Mosquitoes Buzz in People's Ears
Retold by Verna Aardema
Pictures by Leo and Diane Dillon (Dial)

1975—Arrow to the Sun
Gerald McDermott (Viking)

1974—Duffy and the Devil
Retold by Harve Zemach
Pictures by Margot Zemach (Farrar)

1973—The Funny Little Woman
Lafcadio Hearn, retold by Arlene Mosel
Illustrated by Blair Lent (Dutton)

1972—One Fine Day
Nonny Hogrogian (Macmillan)

1971—A Story A Story
Gail E. Haley (Atheneum)

1970—Sylvester and the Magic Pebble
William Steig (Windmill Books)

1969—The Fool of the World and the Flying Ship
Retold by Arthur Ransome
Illustrated by Uri Shulevitz (Farrar)

1968—Drummer Hoff
Adapted by Barbara Emberly
Illustrated by Ed Emberley (Prentice-Hall)

Caldecott Medal Winners

1967—Sam, Bangs & Moonshine
Evaline Ness (Holt)

1966—Always Room for One More
Sorche Nic Leodhas
Illustrated by Nonny Hogrogian (Holt)

1965—May I Bring a Friend?
Beatrice Schenk de Regniers
Illustrated by Beni Montresor (Atheneum)

1964—Where the Wild Things Are
Maurice Sendak (Harper)

1963—The Snowy Day
Ezra Jack Keats (Viking)

1962—Once a Mouse
Marcia Brown (Scribner)

1961—Baboushka and the Three Kings
Ruth Robbins
Illustrated by Nicolas Sidjakov (Parnassus)

1960—Nine Days to Christmas
Marie Hall Ets and Aurora Labastida (Viking)

1959—Chanticleer and the Fox
Barbara Cooney (Crowell)

1958—Time of Wonder
Robert McCloskey (Viking)

1957—A Tree is Nice
Janice Udry
Illustrated by Marc Simont (Harper)

1956—Frog Went A-Courtin'
Retold by John Langstaff
Illustrated by Feodor Rojankovsky (Harcourt)

1955—Cinderella
Illustrated and retold from Perrault by Marcia
Brown (Scribner)

1954—Madeline's Rescue
Ludwig Bemelmans (Viking)

1953—The Biggest Bear
Lynd Ward (Houghton)

1952—Finders Keepers
Will Lipkind
Illustrated by Nicolas Mordvinoff (Harcourt)

1951—The Egg Tree
Katherine Milhous (Scribner)

1950—Song of the Swallows
Leo Politi (Scribner)

1949—The Big Snow
Berta and Elmer Hader (MacMillan)

1948—White Snow, Bright Snow
Alvin Tresselt
Illustrated by Roger Duvoisin (Lothrop)

1947—The Little Island
Golden MacDonald
Illustrated by Leonard Weisgard (Doubleday)

1946—The Rooster Crows
Maude and Miska Petersham (Macmillan)

1945—Prayer for a Child
Rachel Field
Illustrated by Elizabeth Orton Jones
(Macmillan)

1944—Many Moons
James Thurber
Illustrated by Louis Slobodkin (Harcourt)

1943—The Little house
Virginia Lee Burton (Houghton)

1942— Make Way for Ducklings
Robert McCloskey (Viking)

1941—They Were Strong and Good
Robert Lawson (Viking)

1940—Abraham Lincoln
Ingri and Edgar Parin d'Aulaire (Doubleday)

1939—Mai Li
Thomas Handforth (Doubleday)

1938—Animals of the Bible
Helen Dean Fish
Illustrated by Dorothy P. Lathrop (Lippincott)

Newbery Medal Winners

The *Newbery Medal*, named for eighteenth-century British bookseller John Newbery, is awarded annually by the Association for Library Service to Children, a division of the American Library Association, to the *author* of the most distinguished contribution to American literature for children. The award began in 1922.

1991—Maniac Magee
Jerry Spinelli (Little, Brown)

1990—Number the Stars
Lois Lowry (Houghton Mifflin)

1989—Joyful Noise
Paul Fleischman (Harper Row)

1988—Lincoln: A Photobiography
Russell Freedman (Houghton)

1987—The Whipping Boy
Sid Fleischman (Greenwillow)

1986—Sarah, Plain and Tall
Patricia MacLachlan (Harper)

1985—The Hero and the Crown
Robin McKinley (Greenwillow)

1984—Dear Mr. Henshaw
Beverly Cleary (Morrow)

1983—Dicey's Song
Cynthia Voigt (Atheneum)

1982—A Visit to William Blake's Inn: Poems for Innocent and Experienced Travelers
Nancy Willard (Harcourt)

1981—Jacob Have I Loved
Katherine Peterson (Crowell)

1980—A Gathering of Days
Joan W. Blos (Scribner)

1979—The Westing Game
Ellen Raskin (Dutton)

1978—Bridge to Terabithia
Katherine Paterson (Crowell)

1977—Roll of Thunder, Hear My Cry
Mildred D. Taylor (Dial)

1976—The Grey King
Susan Cooper (Atheneum)

1975—M.C. Higgins, the Great
Virginia Hamilton (Macmillan)

1974—The Slave Dancer
Paula Fox (Bradbury)

1973—Julie of the Wolves
Jean Craighead George (Harper)

1972—Mrs. Frisby and the Rats of NIMH
Robert C. O'Brien (Atheneum)

1971—Summer of the Swans
Betsy Byars (Viking)

1970—Sounder
William H. Armstrong (Harper)

1969—The High King
Lloyd Alexander (Holt)

1968—From the Mixed-Up Files of Mrs. Basil E. Frankweiler
E.L. Konigsburg (Atheneum)

1967—Up a Road Slowly
Irene Hunt (Follett)

1966—I, Juan de Pareja
Elizabeth Borton de Trevino (Farrar)

1965—Shadow of a Bull
Maia Wojciechowska (Atheneum)

1964—It's Like This, Cat
Emily Neville (Harper)

1963—A Wrinkle in Time
Madeleine L'Engle (Farrar)

1962—The Bronze Bow
Elizabeth George Speare (Houghton)

1961—Island of the Blue Dolphins
Scott O'Dell (Houghton)

1960—Onion John
Joseph Krumgold (Crowell)

Newbery Medal Winners

1959—**The Witch of Blackbird Pond**
Elizabeth George Speare (Houghton)

1958—**Rifles for Watie**
Harold Keith (Crowell)

1957—**Miracles on Maple Hill**
Virginia Sorensen (Harcourt)

1956—**Carry on, Mr. Bowditch**
Jean Lee Latham (Houghton)

1955—**The Wheel of the School**
Meindert DeJong (Harper)

1954—**…And Now Miguel**
Joseph Krumgold (Crowell)

1953—**Secret of the Andes**
Ann Nolan Clark (Viking)

1952—**Ginger Pye**
Eleanor Estes (Harcourt)

1951—**Amos Fortune, Free Man**
Elizabeth Yates (Dutton)

1950—**The Door in the Wall**
Marguerite de Angeli (Doubleday)

1949—**King of the Wind**
Marguerite Henry (Rand McNally)

1948—**The Twenty-One Balloons**
William Pène du Bois (Viking)

1947—**Miss Hickory**
Carolyn Bailey (Viking)

1946—**Strawberry Girl**
Lois Lenski (Lippincott)

1945—**Rabbit Hill**
Robert Lawson (Viking)

1944—**Johnny Tremain**
Esther Forbes (Houghton)

1943—**Adam of the Road**
Elizabeth Gray (Viking)

1942—**The Matchlock Gun**
Walter Edmonds (Dodds)

1941—**Call It Courage**
Armstrong Sperry (Macmillan)

1940—**Daniel Boone**
James Daugherty (Viking)

1939—**Thimble summer**
Elizabeth Enright (Rinehart)

1938—**The White Stag**
Kate Seredy (Viking)

1937—**Roller Skates**
Ruth Sawyer (Viking)

1936—**Caddie Woodlawn**
Carol Bring (Macmillan)

1935—**Dobry**
Monica Shannon (Viking)

1934—**Invincible Louisa**
Cornelia Meigs (Little, Brown)

1933—**Young Fu of the Upper Yangtze**
Elizabeth Lewis (Winston)

1932—**Waterless Mountain**
Laura Armer (Longmans)

1931—**The Cat Who Went to Heaven**
Elizabeth Coatsworth (Macmillan)

1930—**Hitty, Her First Hundred Years**
Rachel Field (Macmillan)

1929—**The Trumpeter of Krakow**
Eric P. Kelly (Macmillan)

1928—**Gay Neck, the Story of a Pigeon**
Dhan Mukerji (Dufton)

1927—**Smoky, the Cowhorse**
Will James (Scribner)

1926—**Shen of the Sea**
Arthur Chrisman (Dutton)

1925—**Tales from Silver Lands**
Charles Finger (Doubleday)

1924—**The Dark Frigate**
Charles Hawes (Atlantic/Little)

1923—**The Voyages of Doctor Dolittle**
Hugh Lofting (Lippincott)

Information Inventory

Environmental Resources

Contact the following places for more information on environmental topics.

The Aluminum Association
900 19th Street N.W.
Washington, D.C. 20006

American Forestry Association
Global ReLeaf
P.O. Box 2000
Washington, D.C. 20013

The Center for Marine Conservation
1725 Desales Street N.W., Suite 500
Washington D.C., 20036

Citizens for a Better Environment
33 East Congress, Suite 523
Chicago, IL 60605

Creating Our Future
398 North Ferndale
Mill Valley, CA 94941

Earth Care Paper
P.O. Box 3335
Madison, WI 53704

The Ecology Center
2530 San Pablo Avenue
Berkeley, CA 94702

Environmental Action
1525 New Hampshire N.W.
Washington, D.C. 20036

Friends of the Earth
251 Laurier Avenue West, Suite 701
Ottawa, Ontl, Canada K1P 5J6
(for information on global warming or ozone issues)

Greenpeace
1436 U Street N.W.
Washington, D.C. 20009

Greenpeace Canada
578 Bloor Street West
Toronto, Ont., Canada M6G 1K1

The Kids' EarthWorks Group
1400 Shattuck Avenue, Suite 25
Berkeley, CA 94709

The National Audubon Society
645 Pennsylvania Avenue S.E.
Washington, D.C. 20003

Paper Recycling Committee
American Paper Institute
260 Madison Avenue
New York, NY 10016

Recycle for the Birds
National Wildlife Federation
8925 Leesburg Pike
Vienna, VA 22184

Recycling Council of Ontario
489 College Street, Room 504
Toronto, Ont., Canada M6G 1A5

Sierra Club
730 Polk Street
San Francisco, CA 94009

Tree People
12601 Mulholland Drive
Beverly Hills, CA 90210

Worldwatch Institute
1776 Massachusetts Avenue N.W.
Washington, D.C. 20036

World Wildlife Fund
1250 24th Street N.W.
Washington, D.C. 20037

Bone Up on Bones

*Become familiar with the bones that make up the human skeleton.
Use this as a reference page for memory games,
science units and advanced spelling lists.*

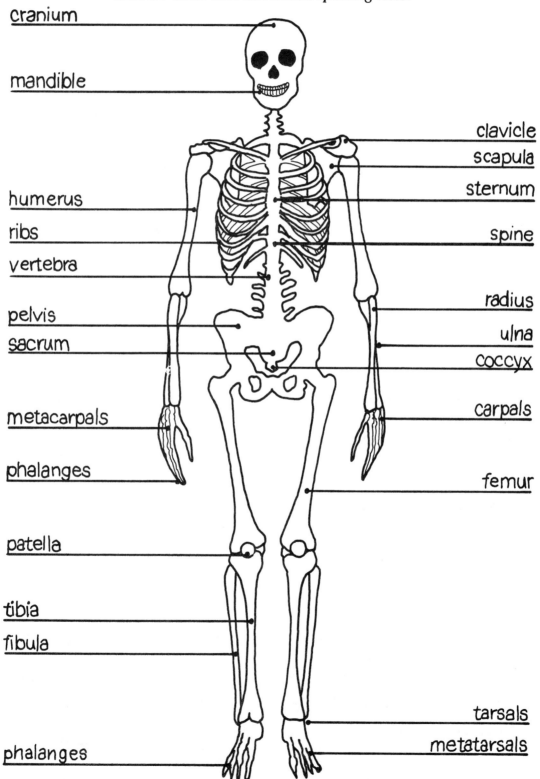

cranium

mandible

clavicle
scapula
sternum

humerus

ribs

spine

vertebra

radius

pelvis

ulna

sacrum

coccyx

metacarpals

carpals

phalanges

femur

patella

tibia

fibula

tarsals

metatarsals

phalanges

Clip-Art Creativity

IDEAS, IDEAS, IDEAS!

Sometimes homemade is the best way! Use your imagination and the clip-art library to create loads of motivating tools for your classroom.

Just cut, paste and photocopy!

With clip-art you can...

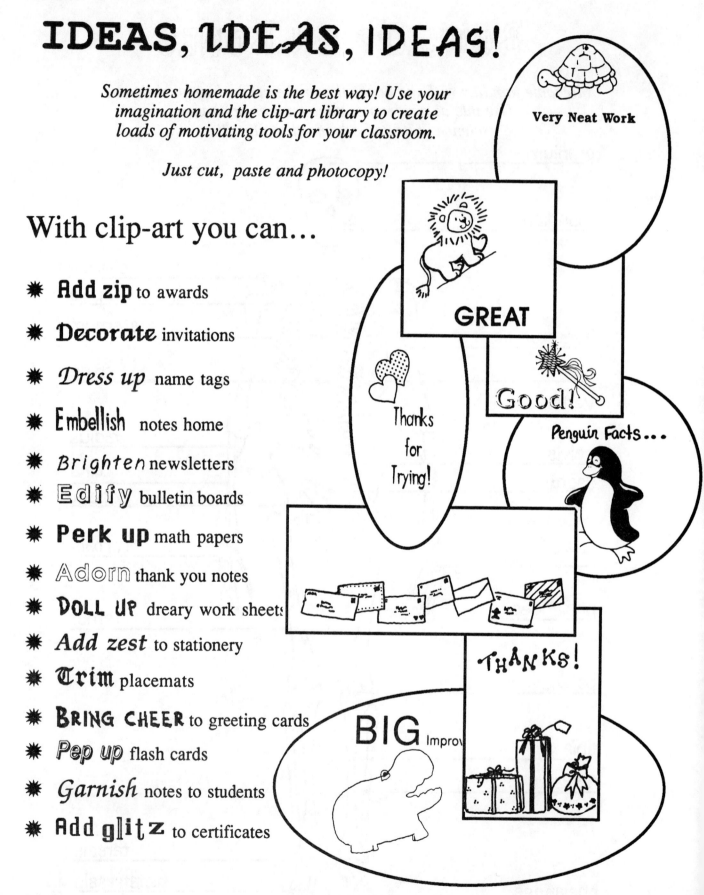

* **Add zip** to awards

* **Decorate** invitations

* *Dress up* name tags

* Embellish notes home

* *Brighten* newsletters

* Edify bulletin boards

* **Perk up** math papers

* Adorn thank you notes

* **DOLL UP** dreary work sheets

* *Add zest* to stationery

* Trim placemats

* **BRING CHEER** to greeting cards

* *Pep up* flash cards

* *Garnish* notes to students

* **Add glitz** to certificates

Very Neat Work

GREAT

Thanks for Trying!

Good!

Penguin Facts...

THANKS!

BIG Improv

Fancy Boxes

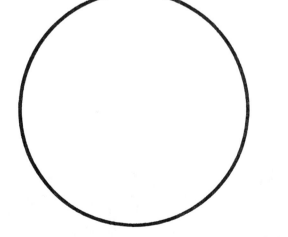

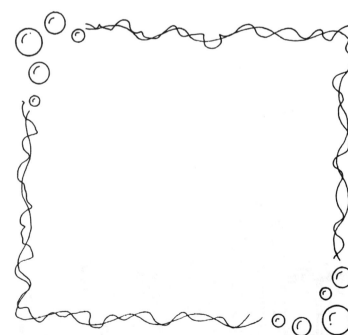

Borders

Borders

Motivating Words

SUPER JOB!

Keep Trying!

GREAT

FABULOUS

Good Work

WOW!

Super Star

Excellent

TERRIFIC TRY

Simply Marvelous

BIG Improvement

Good!

Very Neat Work

Wonderful Work

Thanks for Trying!

GREAT!

Super

Much Better

Stamp of Approval

TOP JOB

FALL

Clip-Art Creativity

Spring

Summer

Halloween

Clip-Art Creativity

Thanksgiving

Clip-Art Creativity
CHRISTMAS

Clip-Art Creativity

Valentine's Day

St. Patrick's Day

Clip-Art Creativity

Hanukkah

Presidents

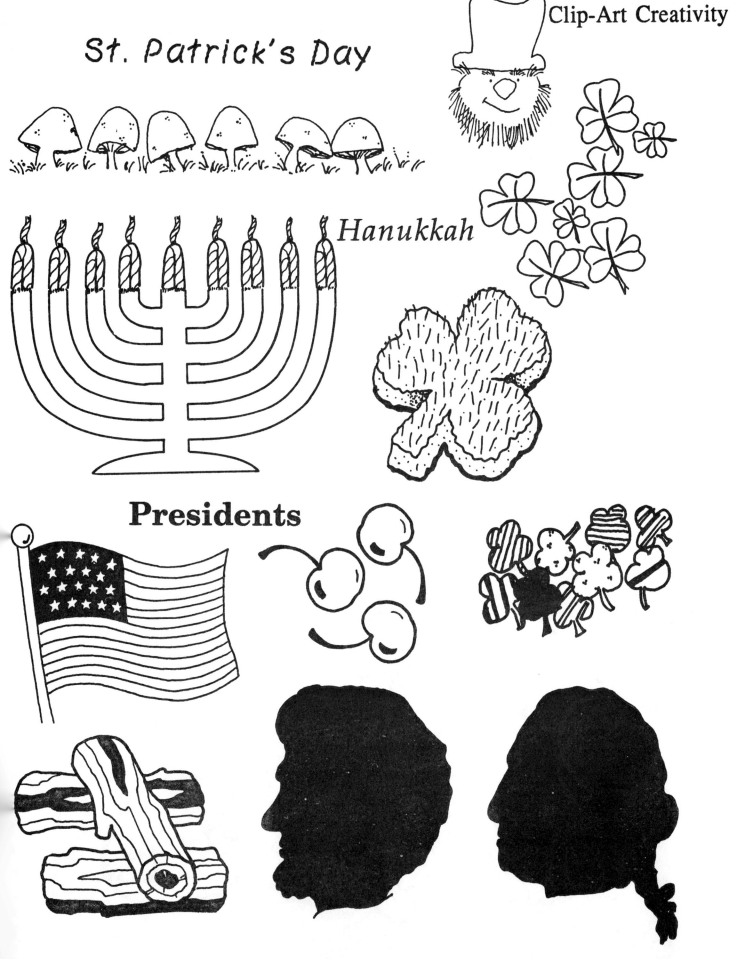

Easter

Transportation

School Things

ALL-PURPOSE GLUE

Clip-Art Creativity

Animals

WORLD ATLAS OF ANIMALS

DINOSAURS

Sports 'n Snacks

Fun Stuff

Index

Index